The Writings of

JOHN

St. John • The Epistles • The Revelation

S. Michael Wilcox

ISBN 1–55517–009–9

Randall Book Company
1182 N. Industrial Park Drive
Orem, UT 84057

Printed in the United States of America

Acknowledgements

My deep and sincere gratitude goes to Dr. Dennis Largey, Assistant Professor of Ancient Scripture of Brigham Young University, for his hours of careful editing and scriptural insight, without which I could not have presented this work with confidence.

CONTENTS

CHAPTER THREE

CHAPTER FOUR

CHAPTER FIVE

CHAPTER SIX

Preface

For years I have loved the writings of John. I have never read his works without coming away edified and amazed at his testimony and the power of his language. Each time I return to his works I find new discoveries awaiting me. I have never been disappointed. In his Gospel, the Epistles, and the Revelation, we find a field of ever–growing wheat which we are invited time and time again to harvest. How, then, can I begin to write an exhaustive commentary on that which is inexhaustive? I have pondered this much and have realized that the attempt would prove disastrous. I have not written an exhaustive commentary. I have barely scratched the surface. I have only taken a few grains of truth from the seashore of John's testimony and held them up for closer observation. I do this in the hope that it may lead readers to find their own grains, sifting the truth through their spiritual fingers, then digging again and again into the shore. I am hoping that the beauty of one or two grains will prompt a search of discovery. We will look at John's writings on only one level. There are many others waiting to be studied.

I also hope that this brief study will help provide the reader with some tools, scriptural shovels, with which one can dig to the very depth of God's truth.

I have chosen to detail an image of Christ given in the following pages because I believe that image has great relevancy to today's church and world. Too many Christians today create their own image of Christ and his Gospel. They write their own definition of what constitutes a true disciple. John brings us out of the fogs generated by our own doctrinal creations. Against the touchstone of his testimony, the fogs melt away in the radiance of Christ's true reality and the reality of his will concerning us.

In regard to the Revelation, the fogs sometimes appear impassable. I do not pretend to understand every image written therein. Only a fool would so pretend, but I believe the images stand for themselves and contain power for us if we will allow them to speak in their own language. I have attempted to explain in part that symbolic language. Once you have learned it, though you speak it as a child, the symbols will continue to widen and clarify, until many heretofore difficult passages of scripture begin to reveal their secrets.

Throughout this commentary, I do not wish to lead the reader to believe that every insight, comparison, and symbol was deliberately placed there by the apostle. All writers know that themes and symbols arise naturally from the written word, particularly writing done under the inspiration of the Holy Ghost. There is a very real limit placed on us today as we try to understand what went on in the mind of John as he wrote under inspiration. This commentary does not wish to impose a strict interpretation, but hopes to give added insight through a careful analysis of words and themes.

Now, a final caution. This commentary was not written to be read alone, but in conjunction with the scriptures. *The focus should be on the scriptures which should constitute the **main study**.* If read alone, this book's effect will be practically nullified. Only the scriptures give life. Commentaries, at best, are microscopes to examine the text better. At all costs we must not make the tool more important than the word.

May I conclude with one last thought? I have hanging on my wall a quotation by Gordon B. Hinkley. I read it almost everyday.

> I do not claim distinction as a scholar of the scriptures. The reading of our scripture, for me, is not the pursuit of scholarship. Rather it is a love affair with the word of the Lord and that of His prophets.

I echo these sentiments. I have found the scriptures reveal their truths much easier under the gentle eyes of love, pondering, reflection, and the whisperings of the spirit, than the sometimes blunt objectivity of scholarship. I respect scholarship, but have found other tools with sharper edges. You do not need to be a great scholar to discover worlds of meaning in God's holy books, but you must love them and allow the spirit to speak

through that love. I have not yet discovered a
sharper tool than this.

S.M.W.

CHAPTER ONE

The Life of John

Before examining the writings of the Apostle John, it would be advantageous to summarize what we know about him. By gleaning episodes from the Gospels and modern revelation, we can gain a beginning view, if not a comprehensive one, of John's character. His writings themselves will provide the best clues to an understanding of John, for out of a man's heart true personality can be judged. It will be helpful, however, to document what we know of the life of John.

By applying the vision Abraham had of "the intelligences that were organized before the world was"; we can conclude that John was a "great and noble" premortal spirit (Abraham 3:22–23). In that world he was foreordained to come forth in the meridian of time to stand with the Savior as one of his special witnesses. The type of individual preparation this required we are not told, but we can be confident that in the premortal world John chose righteousness and good works.

John was born to a Galilean family. His father was a man named Zebedee. His brother,

James, would stand with John in the council of three apostles closest to Christ. The first information we are given about John is his acquaintance with John the Baptist. John, and in all probability James also, were followers of John the Baptist before they followed Jesus. In John 1:35-37 we read of John's first meeting with Christ.

> Again the next day after John stood, and two of his disciples:
> And looking upon Jesus as he walked, he saith, Behold the Lamb of God!
> And the two disciples heard him speak, and they followed Jesus.

Andrew is named as one of the disciples and though John is not mentioned specifically, it is generally accepted that the unnamed disciple throughout the Gospel is the writer himself.

Such was the faith of John in the Baptist that he followed Christ immediately upon hearing the Baptist's testimony. As the other early Apostles, John believed in the messiahship of Jesus and followed him without first seeing miracles and signs. The above verse indicates that John was also an acquaintance of Andrew, for he identifies him as one of the two disciples. Therefore, in all probability, he was a friend of Peter also, for Peter and Andrew were brothers. All of them were from Galilee.

John and his brother James, were fishermen by profession. Mark tells us they were engaged in mending their nets when Christ called them to his permanent service.

> And straightway he called them: and they left their father Zebedee in the ship with the hired servants, and went after him (Mark 1:20).

The willingness to leave all to follow the Master shows the degree of sacrifice that was a part of John's character. We can assume that John was fairly well established as a fisherman for the family had "hired servants" under their employ. There is also the probability that John's family held a respected place in Jewish society. At least he was known by the high priest. During the trial of Jesus, John was permitted entrance into the palace of the high priest because "that disciple was known unto the high priest." His influence was such that he could speak "unto her that kept the door" and bring in Peter (John 18:15, 16).

John was selected by Christ to witness some events not seen by the other Apostles. He, with Peter and James, constituted a First Presidency of the early church. He was present when Christ raised the daughter of Jairus to life. He was privileged to see the Master transfigured on the mountain, standing with Elijah and Moses. He heard the voice of the Father declare, "This is my beloved Son in whom I am well pleased; hear ye him" (Matthew 17:5). When relating this event, Joseph Smith expressed, "The Savior, Moses and Elias gave the keys (of the priesthood) to Peter, James and John, on the mount when they were transfigured before him" (*Teachings of the Prophet Joseph Smith*, pg. 158). Apparently John not only saw the Transfiguration of Christ in his glory, he shared some of that glory and received priesthood keys.

We learn something else about the visions John saw on the mount in the Doctrine and Covenants.

> Nevertheless, he that endureth in faith and doeth my will, the same shall overcome, and shall receive an inheritance upon the earth when the day of transfiguration shall come;
> When the earth shall be transfigured, even according to the pattern which was shown unto mine apostles upon the mount; of which account the fulness ye have not yet received (D&C 63:20–21).

Thus John saw a pattern of the Transfiguration of the earth when it will be renewed and become the inheritance of those who have endured.

At the close of Jesus' life, when his "hour" had come, John was permitted to enter the garden with Peter and James. He does not relate the events or suffering that took place there. Perhaps he felt the other gospel writers testified of that moment sufficiently. Perhaps it was a moment of such sacredness that John did not attempt to describe it. We know his weariness caused him to sleep as the night continued. There may have been other unrecorded moments where the Savior, in close intimacy with his chosen three Apostles shared truth and the spirit.

John was not a perfect human being. He needed to develop his character, understanding and faith like all men. Christ surnamed James and John, "the sons of thunder." There may be general reasons for this name, but whatever they are, the name tends to dispel an often prevailing notion that John was effeminate. On one occasion Luke tells us James and John asked Jesus if he wanted them to call down fire from heaven to destroy a Samaritan village that refused to receive Christ. This lack of understanding and harsh judgment brought a swift rebuke from the Savior.

> But he turned, and rebuked them, and said, Ye know not what manner of spirit ye are of.
>
> For the Son of man is not come to destroy men's lives, but to save them. And they went to another village (Luke 9:55–56).

On another occasion John came to Christ saying, "Master, we saw one casting out devils in thy name, and he followeth not us: and we forbad him, because he followeth not us." Jesus once again gently corrected his intense and loyal Apostle with the following words.

> But Jesus said, Forbid him not: for there is no man which shall do a miracle in my name, that can lightly speak evil of me.

For he that is not against us is on our part (Mark 9:39–40).

Shortly after this event James and John came to Christ saying:

> ...Master we would that thou shouldest do for us whatsoever we shall desire.
> And he said unto them, What would ye that I should do for you?
> They said unto him, Grant unto us that we may sit, one on thy right hand, and the other on thy left hand, in thy glory.
> But Jesus said unto them, Ye know not what ye ask: can ye drink of the cup that I drink of? and be baptized with the baptism that I am baptized with?
> And they said unto him, *We can.* And Jesus said unto them, Ye shall indeed drink of the cup that I drink of; and with the baptism that I am baptized withal shall ye be baptized:
> But to sit on my right hand and on my left hand is not mine to give; but it shall be given to them for whom it is prepared (Mark 10:35–40).

This desire caused animosity among the other apostles and was the catalyst of Christ's teaching of the need for service by those who would be "great among you." And yet there is great power in their simple testimony—"We can."

From these experiences John is seen learning to overcome human weakness. We see a fierce, very deep loyalty to Christ, but often a misunderstanding of his true role. Perhaps this is why, years later he wrote his Gospel, he focused so intently on helping his readers see Christ's true mission and character.

This intense loyalty may partially explain why John was "beloved" of the Savior. In John's writings, however, we perceive a gentle, meek apostle, still fiercely loyal to Jesus, but filled with a compassion and depth of charity that are evident of his realization of Christ's true will, mission, and personality. John evidently learned to follow his Master well. As he associated with Christ, his character matured and he reflected the Master more perfectly.

Of all the Apostles, John seems to be the most sensitive. John is the first to "believe" in the resurrected Christ even before he had seen him and touched his hands and feet. He is the first to recognize the resurrected Savior on the shore of the Sea of Galilee after the repetition of the miracle of the multitude of fishes. Perhaps these aspects of his character are clues to help us understand why he was the "beloved" disciple.

John, with Peter, prepared the Last Supper and John was seated next to the Savior during that supper. To John, Christ confided the knowledge that Judas would betray him. After the arrest in the Garden of Gethsemane John did not leave his Master, but followed the arresting party into the palace of Caiaphas. From his careful recording of the conversation between Pilate and Jesus, we might conclude he was also present during the Roman trial. We know he was present at the crucifixion, perhaps the only Apostle who witnessed it. So great was the confidence of Christ in John that from his agony on the cross he gave John charge concerning his mother, Mary. We are told that "from that hour that disciple took her into his own home" (John 19:27). This last act denotes the level of confidence Christ had in John, and John's sensitive, caring nature.

John was the first Apostle to run to the tomb when the women announced the body of Christ was gone. His reverent waiting at the tomb entrance until Peter arrived is consistent with his character. In words of simple testimony he declares:

> Then went in also that other disciple, which came first to the sepulchre, and *he saw, and believed* (John 20:8).

In contrast to others who needed to see the literal resurrected Christ, John's faith stands unique.

At the sea of Galilee John was asked:

> And the Lord said unto me: John, my beloved, what desirest thou? For if you shall ask what you will, it shall be granted unto you (D&C 7:1).

On this occasion John requested the privilege of having "power over death that I may live and bring souls unto thee." His request shows his grasp of the full purposes of both the Father and the Son and the depth of love and commitment John had to them and to his fellowman, the Lord's sheep. His request was granted. Christ told Peter,

> ...I will make him [John] as flaming fire and a ministering angel; he shall minister for those who shall be heirs of salvation who dwell on the earth (D&C 7:6).

With these desires of John in mind, it is little wonder he spoke frequently and movingly about the need for love.

Having received this promise John began his ministry after the resurrected Christ's ascension. He was present with Peter at the healing of the lame man. He stood boldly before the Jewish leaders bearing testimony with Peter of the divine sonship of Christ, declaring: "We cannot but speak the things which we have seen and heard" (Acts 4:20). He was later beaten for refusing to silence his testimony.

John, with the other apostles, spread the gospel throughout the ancient world. He was banished to the Isle of Patmos for his testimony, where he was shown the great revelation that is now the last book of the Bible. The beauty of the imagery of that book along with the symbolic depth and power of testimony in his Gospel and Epistles prove John as a master of literature. And though he was described as being "unlearned and ignorant," the Holy Ghost gave him power of expression and depth beyond the power of men. His writings have gone down in history as some of the most sublime of all time.

Tradition places John in Ephesus during the latter days of his life. When the dark mists of apostasy settled over the early Church, John fought for its purity until the Lord took him (like the three Nephites) from the Church and he began his centuries long ministry promised him by Christ at the Sea of Galilee. Of his long ministry we know very little. Joseph Smith taught that John was working among the lost Ten Tribes of Israel.

> The Spirit of the Lord fell upon Joseph in an unusual manner, and he prophesied that John the Revelator was then among the Ten tribes of Israel who had been led away by Shalmaneser, king of Assyria, to prepare them for their return from their long dispersion, to again possess the land of their fathers (*History of the Church, Vol. 1*, pg. 176).

We know that John came with Peter and James to the Prophet Joseph Smith and Oliver Cowdery in 1829 to restore the Melchizedek Priesthood. We can be sure that John's ministry will continue until the second coming of the Lord, prior to the millenium. The Doctrine and Covenants describes John's role in that coming in the following words:

> And again, verily, verily, I say
> unto you, and it hath gone forth in a
> firm decree, by the will of the Father,
> that mine apostles, the Twelve which
> were with me in my ministry at
> Jerusalem, shall stand at my right
> hand at the day of my coming in a
> pillar of fire, being clothed with robes
> of righteousness, with crowns upon
> their heads, in glory *even as I am*, to
> judge the whole house of Israel, even
> as many as have loved me and kept my
> commandments, and none else (D&C
> 29:12).

All that have loved the Savior shall know
John and receive righteous judgment or ministry
from him. We can assume that his righteousness
will place him, as Abraham, Isaac and Jacob,
among the gods in fulfillment of his own prophecy
written in his First Epistle.

> Beloved, now are we the sons of
> God, and it doth not yet appear what
> we shall be: but we know that when he
> shall appear, we shall be like him; for
> we shall see him as he is (1 John 3:2).

With this brief life capsule in mind let us
examine John's testimony through the power of his
written word.

CHAPTER TWO

The Gospel of John

John's Vision of Christ

Joseph Smith changed the title of each of the four Gospels from "Gospel" to "Testimony." This changes our view of the Apostles' writings. We are not just reading the "good news" inherent in Christ's teachings and sacrifice. We are receiving four different witnesses, four different testimonies to his divinity. The purpose of a testimony is to strengthen and convert. Each Gospel writer sought to bring his readers to a fuller conviction. This John plainly stated at the conclusion of his testimony.

> But these are written, that ye might believe that Jesus is the Christ, the Son of God; and that believing ye might have life through his name (John 20:31).

Knowing this is John's purpose, achieved through his own personal testimony, we can find a

marvelous pattern developing in his writings. I
believe this pattern was deliberately placed
throughout the Testimony of John, and that he
carefully chose the words and events he would
relate. Even the order of the events he chose to
explain was deliberate to heighten his overall
purpose. This pattern centers on the repeated use
of the verb "to see." Understanding this verb usage
by John and the Master he so frequently quotes, will
help us understand what true conversion and true
discipleship means. John wants his readers to
"see" Christ, for seeing him will convince them
that Jesus is, in truth, the Messiah, the Son of God.
However, the "seeing" John demands requires
more than mere eyesight, for there are many levels
of seeing. It compels spiritual perception and
vision, a seeing that comes through the power of the
Spirit.

JOHN CHAPTER ONE
Come and See

In the preface to John's Gospel we are
introduced to what John wants us to see and the
reason John is able to show it to us. There are a
number of truths about Christ John testifies to in
the first verses of chapter one. We are to see and
understand that Jesus: 1. Taught the gospel "in
the beginning" and "was of God." 2. He was the
"creator of all things." 3. He was the "light" and
"life" of men, a light that "lighteth every man who
cometh into the world." 4. He is "full of grace and
truth." 5. He was the "Lamb of God" sent to make
all men who believe on him "sons of God" and

partakers "of his fulness," through the merits of his Atonement, and 6. To see God the Father is to see and "bear record of the Son," and to see the Son is to know the Father. In short, John wants us to see the divine Son of God, not only the mortal Messiah. John wants us to know that Christ is not only the light we must see, but the light by which we see and know everything else, the light by which we live, "which was the true light, which lighteth everyone who cometh into the world." Without this vision of the Savior, we walk in darkness.

During the preface John introduces one of the main concerns he will deal with throughout his testimony. Christ came into this world of darkness to help us see, but "the world knew him not." The light and life of the world was made flesh "and the world perceiveth it not." The world does not see Christ and because of that they will not come to him and be partakers of his fullness. Throughout the Gospel John gives many examples of those who "knew him not." We will examine these as we proceed.

Because the world "perceiveth not," witnesses are sent and testimonies borne by those who have seen. John introduces us to the first New Testament witness who truly "saw" Christ and was therefore converted. "There was a man sent from God, whose name was John (the Baptist). The same came into the world for a witness, to bear witness of the light...." When asked, "Who art thou?" by the Jews, John the Baptist bore witness of the Savior, heightening the theme John wishes to portray. "There standeth one among you, *whom ye know not*." John wishes us to know him, and records the Baptist's most important words: *"Behold the Lamb of God*, who taketh away the sins of the world." The entire Gospel of John is an invitation to *"Behold the Lamb*," i.e., to *see* Him. This invitation is constantly renewed throughout the chapters.

The preface is then concluded with a final testimony of the Baptist. "And *I saw* and bare record that this is the Son of God." To this testimony John the Beloved adds his own for he did in truth *"Behold the Lamb*." He testifies, "And we *beheld* his glory, the glory as of the Only Begotten of the Father, full of grace and truth." John has established his credentials as a competent witness, capable of showing us the Son for he has truly seen him. Through the rest of his narrative he helps all to *"behold* his glory."

Immediately following this preface John issues what can be called the invitation to behold Christ. He does this by relating the account of the calling of the first disciples. In verse thirty–six of chapter one, John the Baptist turns Andrew and John to the Savior with the repeated words, *"Behold the Lamb of God*." This is both the Baptist's testimony and his exhortation to the disciples to look and believe. They follow Christ. Jesus turns and asks a question John would have all of us ask ourselves, *"What seek ye?"* There is an undertone in this verse suggesting inner search. What are we truly seeking? Andrew and John's answer brings from the Savior the invitation: *"Come and see"* (John 1:38–39).

This invitation is repeated with more depth of interpretation and intensity by Philip. After

receiving the beginning spark of testimony he finds
Nathanael and testifies, "We have found
him...Jesus of Nazareth" (John 1:45). To this
declaration Nathanael asks, "Can there any good
thing come out of Nazareth?" This is a first
example of the worldly opposition or darkness that
does not seek to comprehend the light, but judges
quickly, based on surface understanding. It will be
repeated. It serves as a prelude to all the opposition
the Jews give Christ throughout John's Gospel.
They do not believe "a good thing" came out of
Nazareth. Nathanael will see the Savior and
change his judgment—others will not. To
Nathanael's objection Philip answers, "*Come and
see*" (John 1:45). Nathanael comes, sees, believes,
and receives a promise from Christ: "Thou shalt
see greater things than these" (John 1:50).
Nathanael's eyes have begun to perceive the light.
        Philip's "Come and see," linked with
Christ's earlier invitation, serve as John's
invitation to all to "Come and see." It is the first
step toward a testimony, whether it be one of Christ,
Joseph Smith, or the Book of Mormon. If we
"come," we too have the promise of seeing "greater
things." Those greater things will confirm and
strengthen our testimony until we become a
witness of Christ. What are these "greater things?"
The Savior answers, "Hereafter ye shall *see heaven
open* and the angels of God ascending and
descending upon the Son of man" (John 1:51).
There is an echo here of a portion of John the
Baptist's testimony given earlier in the same
chapter. The Baptist testified:

> And John bare record, saying, I
> saw the Spirit descending from heaven
> like a dove, and it abode upon him.
> And I knew him not: but he that
> sent me to baptize with water, the same
> said unto me, Upon whom thou shalt
> see the Spirit descending, and
> remaining on him, the same is he
> which baptizeth with the Holy Ghost
> (John 1:32–33).

The promise is given, therefore, that we shall see the Son in the fulness of grace and truth as John the Beloved and John the Baptist saw him. With the invitation over, John is now ready to show us the Lord.

Let us seek to understand one more thing about seeing and John's call as an Apostle before we proceed. We sustain our leaders as prophets, seers, and revelators. These are important words. How do they apply to John or anyone who comes in the name of the Lord as an Apostle or prophet? We cannot give a full or detailed explanation of these words in this study, but a few basics may help clarify and substantiate John's credentials as a witness.

What is a prophet? The most basic element, aside from all other connotations and under-standings of this word, is given by John himself in Revelation 19:10. "I am thy fellowservant," an angel declared to John, "and of thy brethren that have the testimony of Jesus: worship God: for the testimony of Jesus is the Spirit of prophecy."

John had this testimony through the witness of the Holy Ghost. We will know true prophets by this spirit for they will always speak under its influence.

What is a seer? Again, we will look only at its most basic definition. The meaning is in the word itself. A seer is one who sees or a see–er. In Moses 6, Enoch is described as a "seer," because, among other things, he "beheld things which were not visible to the natural eye" (Moses 6:36). Seers have spiritual vision. They have "eyes to see." John has these eyes. His Gospel is his attempt to help us gain some of that vision and to see the Savior not with the natural eye.

This brings us to the third word—that of revelator. Again the word itself will give a basic understanding if not a detailed one. A revelator is one who reveals. What does he reveal if not that which he sees with his spiritual eyes? In what spirit will he reveal that which he perceives? He will reveal what he sees in the spirit of prophecy which testifies of Christ. All three words are harmonized even in their most simple definition. When we place the significance of a priesthood call and ordination with these words, (the call of an apostle, as a special witness of Christ), we begin to understand the power of John's testimony. All that we study should be examined with John's divine authority as a prophet, seer, revelator, and Apostle in mind.

JOHN CHAPTER TWO
Manifested Forth His Glory

We do not find the verb "to see" or any of its antecedents in chapter two, yet the theme is still dominant. There are three major sections in chapter two: (1.) The marriage at Cana or the turning of water to wine; (2.) the cleansing of the temple; and (3.) Christ's prophecy of the Resurrection of the "temple" of his body. The basic thrust of the chapter is one of change or the new replacing the old. Those who would see Christ must understand that a new order is to be established. Change is coming.

At the marriage of Cana he changes water to wine. We are told by the governor of the feast, "Thou hast kept the good wine until now." The old "water" is replaced by the new "good wine." Some Bible commentators have suggested this miracle is indicative of the superiority of the "new wine" of the gospel over the "old water" of the Law. For the moment the simple change is enough for our study. What is significant is the result of this miracle upon the disciples. John records that the miracle "*manifested* forth his glory; and his disciples believed on him." The disciples, seeing the miracle, have their faith confirmed.

Christ next cleanses the temple. This also strengthens the disciples faith. The new order is shown cleansing the old. Christ came to cleanse, to make his Father's house "a house of order," and to replace the legalistic ritual of the law of Moses, long since corrupted by apostasy, with the fulness of his word and the higher laws of his gospel.

The conversation with the Scribes and
Pharisees which follow the cleansing suggests a
similar ideaology. "Destroy this temple," Jesus
states, "and in three days I will raise it up" (John
2:19). The temple of Judaism, the center of Jewish
worship, will be superceded by the resurrection of
Christ's temple, that of his own body. The worship
associated with a building—the temple, which can
be destroyed and will be within a few decades, will
be replaced by the worship of Christ whose "temple"
shall never be destroyed but will be a constant
witness of the power of the Resurrection that he
promises all mankind. Even the disciples don't see
this truth until the actual Resurrection for it is
beyond their experience. After the Resurrection
they remember his words.

> When therefore he was risen
> from the dead, his disciples
> remembered that he had said this unto
> them; and they believed the scripture,
> and the word which Jesus had said
> (John 2:22).

We are then told by John that "many believed
in his name when they saw the miracles which he
did." However, "...Jesus did not commit himself
unto them..." (John 2:23–24). Their faith came
from seeing miracles, not from seeing the Son of
God. Throughout the rest of the Gospel, John
wants us to see beyond the miracle to the reality it
represents. This is an important theme. He
chooses his miracles with great care. True
conversion will not come as a result of seeing

miracles. One must see the Son. The miracle is a signpost to signify we are on the right road. If we are on the wrong road, it serves as a warning. We must remember that the disciples, whose faith was confirmed and strengthened by the miracle at Cana, already believed he was the Messiah. They bore witness to that truth in chapter one.

JOHN CHAPTER THREE
Light Is Come Into the World

The newness of Christ's gospel in the Jewish world carries over into chapter three in the conversation with Nicodemus, and in the conversation of John the Baptist with his disciples. These two conversations constitute all of chapter three. In the teachings of Christ to Nicodemus and of John the Baptist to his disciples, we observe once again the deliberate use of the verb "to see." Nicodemus comes by night so that he will not be seen. He acknowledges Christ as a "teacher come from God," (John 3:2) because he has seen the miracles. John has already told us the Savior's attitude toward those who "saw the miracle" and believed. Christ's first statement to Nicodemus teaches that all men must themselves become new in order to see the kingdom of God. He states, "Verily, verily, I say unto thee, Except a man be born again, he cannot *see* the kingdom of God" (John 3:3). Seeing the Savior, his kingdom, and being converted requires a change in the individual. One must become new. If one is not willing to make the change, to be born again of the water and spirit one cannot clearly see these truths.

But if one is willing to change, to be born again and make covenants through baptism, the Holy Ghost is given as a constant companion. Through his influence we can see and know all things. We can especially see the Savior more clearly for the Holy Ghost testifies of Christ and cleanses us.

Nicodemus does not understand, or he pretends not to understand, because it would mean giving up the old tradition that he was already part of the Kingdom by virtue of his birth in the family of Abraham. But a new birth is required, a rebirth into the family or Kingdom of Christ. The rebirth precedes seeing fully for without it one cannot receive the gift of the Holy Ghost. However, initial seeing or faith in Christ leads to the rebirth through repentance and humility. Christ says, "Marvel not that...ye [a child of Abraham] must be born again." This statement is followed by an illustration of what it means to be born of the Spirit.

> The wind bloweth where it listeth, and thou hearest the sound thereof, but canst not tell whence it cometh, and whither it goeth: so is every one that is born of the Spirit (John 3:8).

One who is born of the spirit will not be detected or seen in outward ways or rites like circumcision. The new birth can only be seen in the spirit. One can see the wind's effect on outward objects. One will see a born again person by his actions and attitudes. These will indicate the presence of the spirit, the presence of a new man, born of God. When Nicodemus further questions, "How can these things be?" Christ answers with his own testimony, "We...testify that we have *seen*; and ye receive not our witness" (John 3:11).

Christ then bears to Nicodemus a further witness, explaining to him what he must see in order to believe and be born again. "And as Moses lifted up the serpent in the wilderness, even so must the Son of man be lifted up" (John 3:14). Christ sees his mission clearly. Nicodemus must also see it in order to believe, but the concept of a "lifted up" or crucified Messiah is foreign to Nicodemus. He does not see that the Messiah must die, that his death will bring the anticipated salvation. Nicodemus, representing the Jews, looks for another type of Messiah, one who follows more closely the anticipated, traditional Messiah, one who would liberate them from Rome and solve their temporal problems. Jesus corrects this traditional expectation of the Messiah by saying:

> For God so *loved* the world, that he gave his only begotten Son, that whosoever believeth in him should not *perish*, but have everlasting life.
>
> For God sent not his son into the world to *condemn* the world; but that the world through him might be saved.
>
> He that believeth on him is *not condemned*: but he that believeth not is condemned already, because he hath not believed in the name of the only begotten Son of God (John 3:16–18).

Christ came to save "whosoever" believed in him—Greek, Roman, Samaritan, etc. He did not come to condemn or destroy. Those who cannot see this are the ones who will be condemned. "He that believeth not is condemned already...."

Christ concludes his discussion with Nicodemus by expressing the reason why men will not see: "Men loved darkness rather than light, because their deeds were evil." Christ follows by explaining those who do evil stay away from the light "lest their deeds should be reproved." One who does good will come to the light that "his deeds may be manifest." Christ is the light. In his light all actions are seen clearly. The entire conversation revolves around seeing. It also provides us with an example of one who does not see or one who struggles to understand the new because of his close ties to the old. John has established an interesting truth with these last words. Everything Christ does is in the open where men can see because his deeds "are wrought in God." This is compared to the deeds of those who oppose him. They are always plotting in secrecy and darkness. Let us look at a few examples. When Judas leaves the Last Supper John states, "...and it was night." The betrayal, an "evil" deed, is done in darkness. When Christ defends himself before Annas he states by contrast:

> ...I spake *openly* to the world; I ever taught in the synagogue, and in the temple, whither the Jews always resort; and *in secret have I said nothing* (John 18:20).

John the Baptist's teachings to his disciples in the last part of chapter three solidifies some of the ideas we have just discussed. "He must increase, but I must decrease," John explains. Christ represents the newness of the everlasting gospel. John exemplifies the last of the old prophetic line that anticipated the new. He ends with a reiteration of Christ's testimony and then adds his own.

> And what he hath *seen* and heard, that he testifieth; and no man receiveth his testimony.
> The Father loveth the Son, and hath given all things into his hand.
> He that believeth on the Son hath everlasting life: and he that believeth not the Son shall *not see* life; but the wrath of God abideth on him (John 3:32, 35–36).

This final testimony echoes Christ's first words to Nicodemus, ("Except a man be born again, he cannot see the kingdom of God,") and broadens them to include "everlasting life." The Joseph Smith Translation renders the words "see life" to read "shall not receive of his fulness." This teaches us the result of "believing on the Son." It tells us what everlasting life encompasses. It encompasses the reception of Christ's fulness, his grace and truth. It closely parallels the preface of chapter one. The power of chapter three lies in the doctrine that a man who "sees" Christ by being born again will also "see" eternal life through the Atonement.

Through obedience to the Savior's saving gospel principles, a "fulness" can be achieved by an individual.   These promises depend on an individual's readiness to become a "new creature" (Mosiah 27:25) by destroying the old natural man. The newborn man of Christ loves the light. The old natural man seeks the darkness. The blessings hinge on seeing, on "cleansing," and on the establishing of "order" in one's own house, the same themes of chapter two.

JOHN CHAPTER FOUR
Come, See a Man

As chapter two builds a foundation for chapter three, in like manner chapter four rests on truths found in three. There are two main divisions in chapter four. The bulk of the chapter deals with the Samaritan woman at the well. The last section relates the story of the healing of the nobleman's son. By placing the story of the Samaritan woman immediately after Nicodemus, John invites the reader to make a comparison. Nicodemus represents the highest of the high in Judean society. He is a Pharisee, a member of the Sanhedrin, a respected child of the covenant and a strict observer of the law. The gift he bestows at the burial of Christ indicates that he is also a man of means (John 19:39).   With his Pharasidic background, Nicodemus has read the scriptures and knows them intimately. Yet to our knowledge, he does not "see" the messiahship of Christ fully enough to openly proclaim his testimony. He is not made new by a spiritual rebirth since he doesn't partake of the new covenant without reservation. His testimony of Christ is not strong enough to bring him fully into the light, though we see him hesitating in the shadows throughout the Gospel of John.

In contrast we have the woman at the well. She represents in many respects the lowest of the low in Jewish society. She is a despised Samaritan and a woman who has lived a tainted life. At present she is living in a state of fornication, if not adultery. Her conversation and questions to Christ indicate she has a limited and very basic knowledge of the scriptures. Yet this woman "sees" the Savior better than Nicodemus. Her perception of him continues to increase as Christ teaches her of the living water he has to offer.

In verse nine the Samaritan woman sees *"a Jew."* She is surprised he would even speak to her. Christ must overcome her defensive prejudice against him, which he accomplishes throughout the dialogue. He subdues her biases by promising her "living water." Jesus continues: "...the water that I shall give him shall be in him a well of water springing up into everlasting life" (John 4:14).

The message John is relating to those of his readers who want to know the truth about Christ is the Savior's ability to quench every thirst, and to give, as we saw earlier, "everlasting life" through the water he offers. The woman sees, at this point only the temporal, just as Nicodemus saw only the temporal birth, not the spiritual rebirth, and the Jews a structural temple, not the temple of Christ's body. But John wants us to see the spiritual. All spiritual thirsts are soothed with the living water of the gospel. ("Whosoever drinketh of the water I shall give him shall never thirst.") These promises follow naturally the exhortation given to Nicodemus to be born again. Those who are reborn will drink the living water from Christ's well. But the woman fails to see beyond the natural. She wants the water "that I thirst not, neither come hither to draw." Christ then approaches her on a level she can comprehend. He talks to her of her husbands.

After Christ's declaration of her present and past matrimonial state she observes, "Sir, I perceive that thou art a *prophet*." Once she saw "a Jew," now she sees "a prophet." She then invites a commentary on a religious debate between the Samaritans and the Jews—that of the proper place to worship. Should true worship of God take place in the temple of Jerusalem (the Jews' holy mountain) or on Mt. Gerizim (the Samaritan's holy mountain)? Christ's answer is, once again, an attempt to place her on a spiritual level. One must "worship the *Father in spirit* and in truth," he teaches her. "For the Father seeketh such to worship him." Christ then follows with an open declaration of his messiahship. "I that speak unto thee *am he*." (We will see this declaration again in the Garden of Gethsemane.)

The woman leaves, with the approach of the disciples, and goes into the city where she repeats John's theme and invitation given in chapter one: "*Come, see* a man, which told me all things that ever I did: *is not this the Christ?*" The "prophet" is now perceived as "*the Christ*." Where Nicodemus failed, the woman at the well succeeded, and though she does not see Christ fully, nor understand his mission, she has accepted him. She is becoming "new." She has begun to drink the living water he offered her.

While she is gone the disciples reach Jesus. They are surprised that he would speak to a Samaritan woman. Christ perceiving their thoughts offers them a challenge. *"Lift up your eyes, and look* on the fields, for they are ready to harvest." They must learn to see beyond the physical, the outward prejudices, and comprehend the saving love of Christ. In this manner they are similar to Nicodemus to whom Christ said: *"Whosoever* believeth in him should...have everlasting life." This promise is even extended to a sinful Samaritan woman. If they will "lift up (their) eyes and look" they will see this wider harvest of souls.

The episode is concluded with the testimony of the other Samaritan villagers who have heard Christ for themselves and "now believe...and know that this is indeed the Christ, the Savior of the world." That world included the despised Samaritans. The Samaritan testimony is also John's. We feel the power of John's personal conviction coming through Samaritan lips. John will often bear testimony through the lips of others who encounter Jesus as he has here with the Samaritans. We will see that John uses a wide variety of witnesses, from John the Baptist to the wicked High Priest that has Christ crucified, from a man born blind to the voice of God the Father. We must always be ready to receive the testimonies John gives, for this is a book of witnesses.

We have now been presented with back–to–back stories of one who does not see and one who does. Separating these stories is John the Baptist's testimony that those who see shall have eternal life and those who don't receive "the wrath of God." Chapters three and four are meant to be read as a whole, unified presentation of truth.

The last part of chapter four relates the healing of the nobleman's son. It can be viewed as a contrast to the people who "saw the miracles" and believed, but to whom Christ would not commit himself. Upon the request of the nobleman to "come down" (to Capernaum) and heal his son, Christ responds, "Except ye see signs and wonders, ye will not believe." This is a mild rebuke, given to test faith, to which the father replies, "Sir, come down ere my child die." Jesus then heals the child in a manner which requires a faith that goes beyond seeing. He tells the man, "Go thy way; thy son liveth. And the man believed...and he went his way." John has given us an example of a man who believes without "seeing signs and wonders." This father accepts the words of Christ alone. The importance of faith before miracles is reinforced in the last chapters of John's Gospel when Christ rebukes Thomas for having demanded sight before he would believe in the Resurrection. The story is also linked to the conversation with Nicodemus read earlier. One must first believe, then one sees more clearly, as Christ taught Nicodemus.

JOHN CHAPTER FIVE
What He Seeth the Father Do

Chapter five tells the story of an invalid man who is healed at the pool of Bethesda, and the subsequent exchange between the Jews and Christ. We will see this pattern again—first the outward miracles, then a discussion which intensifies the major themes. The spiritual truth underlying the healing is found in the repeated use of the word "whole." Christ can make men whole both physically and spiritually. The man Christ heals had been infirm thirty–eight years. Christ asks him, "Wilt thou be made *whole*?" The response comes back, "I have no man...to put me into the pool." There is no one to help him. The man can only think of the outward superstition that the first man into the pool when the water is "troubled" will be healed. Christ, however, can make him *whole*. The Savior tells him to rise and walk. "And immediately the man was made *whole*."

He is later stopped by the Jews. He explains to the Jews why he is carrying his bed on the Sabbath contrary to their law. He states, "He that made me *whole* said take up thy bed and walk." There is strong emphasis on the word "whole" throughout the episode.

Later Christ and the man meet again. At this meeting Christ admonishes the man, "Behold, thou art made *whole*: Sin no more, lest a worse thing come unto thee." Sin makes men infirm, unable to progress. Christ has the ability through his Atonement to make us spiritually "whole". He can take our "infirmities" upon himself if we "sin no more," just as he took away the invalid's infirmities. There is spiritual truth in the story. John would have us see this truth as clearly as we see the Savior's love and compassion. The truth underlying the story is greater than the miracle, and it begins, as the miracle at Cana and the healing of the nobleman's son, to underscore the love and compassion of the Savior which will become the focus of the later half of John's Gospel.

The rest of the chapter revolves around the relationship of the Father and Son. We are here introduced to a great truth John would have us see and one which will grow as the gospel story proceeds. It is taught by Christ as an answer to the criticism of his "making himself equal with God," and from this point on is a major truth in John's testimony. Christ's first statement to the critical Pharisees who condemn him for healing the infirm man on the Sabbath, deals with seeing.

> Verily, verily, I say unto you, The Son can do nothing of himself, but what he seeth the Father do: for what things soever he doeth, these also doeth the Son likewise.
>
> For the Father loveth the Son, and sheweth him all things that himself doeth: and he will shew him greater works than these, that ye may marvel (John 5:19–20).

Christ has only done that which the Father hath done. This statement of relationship is followed by an explanation of the "greater works." They are the works the Savior has seen the Father do and will repeat. They consist of three main works:

> 1) "For as the Father *raiseth up the dead*, and quickeneth them; even so the Son quickeneth whom he will" (John 5:21).
> 2) "For as the Father *hath life in himself*; so hath he given to the Son to have life in himself;" (John 5:26).
> 3) "And hath given him authority to *execute judgment* also, because he is the Son of man" (John 5:27).

Christ has life in himself, with which he will raise the dead and execute judgment on all, just as he raised the impotent man and told him to "sin no more," indicating a judgment and forgiveness of former sins.

There are several levels of seeing that are implied in Christ's testimony—that he does the works of his Father. First, we know that Christ sees the Father, and he sees him clearly. He can therefore reveal his nature to us in his teachings. This is critical and often missed by readers of the New Testament. Second, Christ only does what he has seen the Father do. He can now reveal the Father's nature through his life. Therefore, to see and know Christ is to see and know the Father—both through Christ's teachings and his life. Because of this truth, "all men should honor the Son, even as they honor the Father." This is one of the great truths John wishes the seeker of

testimony to comprehend. We will see it repeated at
the Last Supper in a statement to Philip.

What were the main objectives Jesus came to
accomplish? Certainly he came to bring the
Atonement, but he also came to reveal to mankind
the nature of a Father, separated from his children
by a veil of forgetfulness. Because Christ sees the
Father, he can tell us of his nature, but more than
that, he reveals his nature through his own life and
mission. He does what the Father does, he speaks
what the Father speaks. In the specific case that
brought on this discussion with the Jews, the
Father also would have shown mercy on the
impotent man. He would have raised him up and
exhorted him to "sin no more." John is, therefore,
giving us a promise. If we can reach the point of
truly seeing the Son, we will at the same time
comprehend the Father. If we truly understand
this point, no one would ever feel a deeper love,
understanding, or closeness to Christ than to the
Father.

Christ ends his speech to the Jews by
appealing to four sources that testify of his divinity:
(1.) John the Baptist; (2.) the "works" he does; (3.)
the "Father himself;" and, (4.) the scriptures,
specifically Moses. If the Jews truly saw John the
Baptist, the works, the Father, or the scriptures,
they would also see Christ, and in seeing Christ
would comprehend the Father. This truth,
however, has not yet been grasped even by the
Apostles. The last of this chapter provides a strong
emphasis on witnesses to Christ's divinity.

JOHN CHAPTER SIX
To Whom Shall We Go?

Chapter six is a turning point for those who believe and follow "him because they saw his miracles." It contains the discourse on the bread of life. In this chapter Christ brings his disciples to a choice. They must see the spiritual reality behind all he does and accept him as the Messiah on his terms or reject him. They cannot continue to believe only because of the miracles. That belief will not produce an exalting faith. It is time to understand that his mission is one of spiritual salvation through the Atonement, not temporal salvation through the satisfaction of physical needs and conquests of oppressing legions of Roman soldiers.

The discourse Christ gives on the bread of life in the synagogue of Capernaum is preceded by the feeding of the five thousand. As we saw in chapter five, the outward miracle becomes a springboard for a spiritual truth. From a few small loaves, thousands are fed "as much as they would." After eating "they were filled," and there were still "fragments that remain," enough to fill twelve baskets. The speech that follows asserts that Christ can spiritually feed us as much as we can partake. His "bread of life" will fill us and there will still be fragments left over. Chapter six is a counterpart to chapter four. Not only can Christ fill us with "living water," but also with "the bread of life." These chapters provide us with a deeper meaning behind one of the Beatitudes. "Blessed are they which do hunger and thirst after righteousness for they shall be filled" (Matthew 5:6). If they hunger and thirst they shall be filled with the bread of life and the living water which comes through the ministration of the Holy Ghost. The Holy Ghost testifies of Christ and his Gospel. The people fail to see the spiritual depth, however, thinking only of the power Christ had to solve the day–to–day necessities of life. They want bread, not the bread of life.

After feeding the five thousand, Christ crosses the sea to Capernaum. The multitudes who follow "because they saw the miracles" seek Christ in the synagogue. The day before when he had fed them with the miraculous loaves and fishes, they wanted to "take him by force, to make him a King." Christ's first statements to them in the synagogue are an attempt to bring them to a spiritual commitment.

> Jesus answered them and said, "Verily, verily, I say unto you, Ye seek me, not because ye desire to keep my saying, neither because ye saw the miracles, but because ye did eat of the loaves, and were filled" (John 6:26 JST).

What sadness this must have produced in the Savior. He had so much to give, but they sought "the loaves" that filled them physically. Christ then explains his previous day's miracle with the words, "Labor not for the meat which perisheth, but for that meat which endureth unto everlasting life." Christ is saying "I will not be your kind of king. I will not give you the earthly bread you seek, but the bread that lasts forever."

They ask for a sign "that we may see, and believe thee." The use of the word "see" here indicates true spiritual blindness. They refer to Moses, wanting him to repeat Moses' forty year miracle of manna, and feed them literally. They want to *see* first and then they will believe. Forgotten already is the previous day's miracle which should have been sign enough. Christ answers their blindness, "*I am* the bread of life...But I said unto you, that ye also have *seen me*, and believe not." Christ himself is the sign they ask for, the bread they seek. This is similar to his statement to the Jews that the destruction of the temple of his body and its resurrection three days later would be his sign to them. If the multitude he fed could really see him they would believe. Other signs would not help.

Christ follows this truth with a promise, "Everyone which *seeth* the Son, and believeth on him, may have *everlasting life*; and I will raise him up at the last day." This assertion causes the Jews to murmur. "Is not this Jesus, the son of Joseph, whose father and mother *we know*?" They see a carpenter's son, not the Eternal Father's son. They "*know*" Joseph as Christ's only father. But as Christ asserted in chapter five, if they *knew* the Father, they would also *know* the Son. Their failure to know the Father causes their blindness in recognizing the Son. Later in John's Gospel we will hear Christ pray:

> And this is life eternal, that they
> might know thee the only true God,
> and Jesus Christ, whom thou hast
> sent (John 17:3).

Seeing, eternal life, and knowing the truth concerning Jesus Christ are related just as deeply as the Father and Son are related. John is once again stressing the close relationship of the Father and Son. This relationship and its link with seeing is explained later in the following verses:

> Every man therefore that
> hath...learned of the Father, cometh
> unto me.
> Not that any man hath seen the
> Father, save he which is of God, he
> hath seen the Father (John 6:45–46).

The above statement is followed by Christ's repeated assertion, "I am the bread of life." This second assertion is explained with a plain reference to his coming sacrifice. "The bread that I will give is my flesh which I will give for the life of the world." Christ is clearly teaching them on a spiritual level. He is attempting to help them see the spiritual truth in order for them to believe. He fed them all bread, and they were filled. He desires to feed them his Atonement, his Gospel and his truths, which will fill them with the Holy Ghost.

They respond to this attempt of Christ by murmuring, "This is a hard saying; who can hear it?" Christ then asks, "Doth this offend you? What and if ye shall see the Son of man ascend up where he was before?" If they cannot comprehend the real purpose of his life, if they don't realize he has come to die, to literally "give (his) flesh" what will they think when his hour comes and he ascends to his Father? If they continue to want "a king" their faith will not withstand the blow when that king dies and returns to his Father, and they do not understand the necessity of his death because they seek the temporal breads of the world.

Christ concludes his discourse with a final pronouncement of his desire that they understand him on a spiritual, rather than a temporal level."It is the spirit that quickeneth; the flesh profiteth nothing: the words that I speak unto you, *they are spirit*, and they are life" (John 6:63).

But they could not see Christ as a spiritual Messiah, and they "walked no more with him." A moment of truth has come. The sun is high and hot and those whose roots are not deep, wither. Testimony cannot survive with only a surface understanding. They had never seen him on any deeper level than as a man sent to satisfy temporal needs, a man of miracles. John would have this episode serve as a warning to all who fail to understand the true mission and personality of Jesus.

In a moment of deep poignancy Christ turns to his twelve apostles and asks, "Will ye also go away?" But Peter answers:

...Lord, to whom shall we go?
thou hast the words of eternal life.

> And we believe and are sure that
> thou art that Christ, the Son of the
> living God (John 6:68–69).

Peter represents an important moment in the
conversion process—the moment of *commitment*.
This moment comes when an individual realizes,
as Peter, that *there is no other choice.* The truth
may be "a hard saying," but there is nowhere or no
one else to whom one can go. Jesus is the way. He
brings new birth. He is the bread of life. He gives
the living water. He makes us whole. We must be
nourished by him in his way or starve. Peter knows
there is no other source of nourishment or
wholeness and because he sees this truth he can
commit to it—and there is strength in that
commitment. The roots sink deeper. The Jews still
believe there is another way, the Law of Moses, or
another Messiah; one who will come and be the type
of Savior they want, not the kind they need. An
individual is beginning to truly eat the bread of life
when this moment of commitment comes. Until
that moment most people try to have the best of both
worlds. If we may borrow from a Book of Mormon
image—they try to reach for the spacious building
while holding the iron rod, or they try to redirect the
iron rod to lead to the building. A decision is
needed, a commitment to feast at the tree
regardless of the consequences of that decision, or
to accept the mocking invitations of those who live
in the spacious building of the world.
　　　This concludes the first major section of
John's testimony. He has issued the invitation to
"Come and see." Those who come will behold

Christ "manifest his glory," but they must understand him on a spiritual level, becoming new, born again. If they see the true Christ on that level and change, they will believe enough to commit themselves to his truth. Seeing helps create the commitment and that in turn leads to greater vision. This is more than receiving the witness that Jesus is the Christ. It is the decision to follow him at all costs. Yet as we continue in John, we will understand that even Peter did not yet fully see the "Son of God," nor understand his mission. Therefore his commitment, though strong, was not yet perfect.

JOHN CHAPTER SEVEN
Search and Look

Chapter seven is one that serves as a touchstone to get our bearings straight. It consists of three divisions: Christ's dialogue with his brothers, his defense before the Jews at the feast, and the debates of the rulers with Nicodemus.

The first verses restate the theme of seeing. Christ's "brethren" urge him to walk openly among the Jews. We are told by John that after the confrontation detailed in chapter six, "Jesus walked in Galilee for he would not walk in Jewry" (meaning Judea). Christ's brothers tell him,

> ...go into Judea, that thy disciples may see the works that thou doest. For there is no man that doeth anything in secret, and he himself seeketh to be known openly. If thou do

these things, shew thyself to the world
(John 7:4).

The statement of the brothers has a depth of
irony that needs examining.   Remember what
Christ said to Nicodemus about evil and good deeds.
Good deeds were done openly in the light that men
might see them and know the man's works were
"wrought in God."   Evil deeds were done in the
darkness, in secret.   At the surface the brothers
seem to be saying to Christ what he said to
Nicodemus: if your deeds are good, show them. We
have already seen that a major difference between
Christ and the Jewish leaders is the openness of
Christ and the secrecy of the Pharisees.   Nowhere
is this more prominent than in the arrest and trial
of Christ in the darkness of night in order to avoid
an "uproar among the people."   There is a subtle
temptation in the brothers' words, almost an
attempt to use his own teachings against him.
Whether this is overtly intentional on the part of the
brothers or not, we cannot tell, but the implication
is clear.   The brothers want him to "shew (himself)
to the world: in the temporal way the world wishes
to accept him.   But as John repeatedly stresses,
miracles and works seen "openly" do not bring a
man to the point where he truly "knows" the
Master. The Savior does not submit to the tempting
suggestion, but remains steady on his course.
Chapter seven, therefore, commences with a
challenge given to Christ to show himself to the
world in the way the world wants, not in the way
the world needs.   Chapter seven builds naturally
upon chapter six.

From this point on, the blindness of the world represented by the opposing Jews, becomes dominant. The Savior understands clearly the brothers' suggestion and responds quickly. "The world cannot hate you, but me it hateth because I testify of it, that the works therefore are evil. " The irony continues in this exchange. The world wants to "see the works" of Christ. Christ came to show the world its own evil works, that it might repent and receive true sight through his Atonement. Their own works the world does not want to see, but in the light that Christ both is and brings, all things are seen clearly, especially the evil which is and will be done "in secret." This continues the echo of the last words of Christ to Nicodemus when he said:

> For every one that doeth evil hateth the light, neither cometh to the light, lest his deeds should be reproved (John 3:20).

The brethren want Christ to show his works so he can be judged of the world or accepted by it. They do not realize they stand in the presence of the world's judge, one who sees and knows all the evil that the world wishes would remain in the dark.

The second section of this chapter tells us the various judgments the world pronounces on Christ. It is a section of debate and division. "...How knoweth this man letters having never learned?" they argue. They judge him by their own worldly standards of learning. Where did he get his knowledge and wisdom since he didn't get it from us? they say. The thought is clear. How can a man teach unless he has been officially trained for the ministry in the worldly way? The debate continues.

> Howbeit we know this man whence he is: but when Christ cometh, no man knoweth whence he is.
> Others said, this is the Christ. But some said, Shall Christ come out of Galilee?
> So there was a division among the people because of him (John 7:27, 41, 43).

Once more irony is a key element, the irony of the true judge *of* the world being judged *by* the world with its unlawful magistrates. In other words, the defendant has placed the judge in the dock and condemned him, claiming to "know whence he is." Notice how deep the irony becomes. They state that when the true Christ comes "no man knoweth whence he is." The implication suggested by the leaders revolves around the fact that they know Jesus' background as a Galilean carpenter. Their statement is, however, true and is literally being fulfilled by their own words. The Christ is standing in front of them and they do not know from whence he comes. Their own blindness fulfills their traditional interpretation of prophecy.

In the center of these "debates" we read Christ's words. They serve as John's commentary and the central message of chapter seven.

> Judge not according to the
> appearance, but judge righteous
> judgment (John 7:24).

The Jews are still not seeing the true Christ.
They are blinded by "traditions." They are looking
only at the temporal, ignoring the spiritual truth
(see JST, vs. 24). Jesus later says, "Ye shall seek
me and shall not find me; and where I am, thither
ye cannot come." They will not find him because
their traditions lead them to wrong places and in
the wrong way. They truly do not know "whence he
is" nor do they know where he is going, as we shall
see later.

John knew the debates concerning Christ
(who he was, and what his mission was) would
rage for centuries. Men would seek him and not
truly find him because they would judge
unrighteously, according to "appearance." He,
therefore, ends chapter seven with a reiteration of
his first invitation. Ironically it comes from the
mouths of those who are Christ's most bitter
enemies, those who claim to "know" him.

The third section of chapter seven contains a
dialogue between the Sanhedrin and Nicodemus.
The officers sent to arrest Jesus have returned
empty handed saying, "Never man spake like this
man." The Pharisees claim the people and officers
are deceived, and contemptuously dismiss those
"who *knoweth* not the law." It is obvious, however,
that they know more than their leaders.
Nicodemus contributes to the judging and knowing
themes by saying, "Doth our law (which the
Sanhedrin claims to know) judge any man before it

hear him and *know* what he doeth?" With contempt they answer Nicodemus, "Art thou also of Galilee? *Search, and look*: for out of Galilee ariseth no prophet." This dovetails perfectly with Nathanael's statement to Philip, "Can there any good thing come out of Nazareth?" Philip's answer was, "Come and see." The Pharisees "*search and look*" issues the same invitation. John has returned us to his major purpose. He is ready in the next chapters to help us "search and look," and in looking, believe.

The Sanhedrin, however, will not believe because they will not follow their own challenge to "search and look." If we remember Christ's statement made earlier in the same chapter, "Ye shall seek me and shall not find me" the irony and power of chapter seven becomes complete both for their day and our own. Why will they not find him? John's answer is, "Because they will not look."

There is one final note I wish to draw attention to in chapter seven. There is a subtle change that takes place at this juncture of the Savior's life. We sense a greater urgency on the part of the Savior to help his listeners accept him. He knows his "hour" is drawing near. We can feel this urgency as John tells us Jesus "*cried*" in the temple as he taught, saying:

> Ye both know me and ye know whence I am: and I am not come of myself, but he that sent me is true, whom ye know not.
> But I know him: for I am from him, and he hath sent me (John 7:28).

Notice once again the emphasis and the irony on knowing, and the Father/Son relationship. We hear the same urgency a few verses later. "Jesus stood and *cried* saying, If any man thirst, let him come unto me and drink." This same urgency on the part of the Savior is felt throughout the remainder of John's Gospel. It is an indication of the Savior's love and the desire he felt that all come to him in order to "walk in the light," and drink from his living water.

JOHN CHAPTER EIGHT
I Am the Light of the World

Chapter eight begins with the episode of the woman taken in adultery and the question concerning her stoning. Christ answers the Pharisees tempting question, "What sayest thou?" with a question of his own. "He that is without sin among you let him first cast a stone at her." When their consciences condemn them and they leave, one by one, Jesus sends the woman away saying, "Neither do I condemn thee, go, and sin no more." Christ's right to judge and forgive is taught here. He judges with wisdom and compassion. He not only judged the woman, but more importantly, her accusers. This is a perfect example of Christ's statement given in chapter seven when he challenged the Pharisees by saying, "Judge not according to the appearance, but judge righteous judgment." He has just given righteous judgment both for the woman and her accusers. Once again we see a logical flow from chapter to chapter.

So far John has shown us that Christ brings rebirth. He gives us living water. He gives us the bread of life until we are filled. He makes us whole. Now John teaches us he can forgive sins and bring righteous judgment. Jesus' following statement, as if in commentary to what has just taken place, is, "I am the light of the world." It is an invitation to follow his example. If we recognize this message and follow it we "shall not walk in darkness." The message is clear. We must forgive as he has. We must judge as he has, and we will be able to do so if we walk in the light of his gospel and example.

The rest of chapter eight is a detailed conversation with the Pharisees, centering around fatherhood. John continues to stress the closeness of Jesus to the Father, for the Father is the source of all that Christ is, does, and says. This major theme, first introduced in the preface and heightened in chapter five, continues to build throughout John's testimony. It is one of the most important aspects of Christ John wants us to see. From this point on John stresses the relationship of the Father and Son constantly.

In chapter eight Christ repeats the same message of chapter five. "The Father that sent me beareth witness of me." He also returns to the message given in the previous chapter. "I know whence I came and whither I go, but ye cannot tell whence I come and whither I go. Ye judge after the flesh...." Christ knows he comes from the Father and goes to the Father. He will later plainly declare this truth.

In the same conversation Christ bears witness that he only teaches those things "which I have heard of him," meaning the Father. He continues by saying, "as my Father taught me I speak these things." This is followed by Christ's concluding testimony of his relationship with the Father. "I do always those things that please him." One of those things that will please the Father will be his atoning sacrifice. Christ alludes to this sacrifice with the following words, "After ye have lifted up the Son of man." This is a clear prophecy concerning the coming crucifixion. All these truths are missed by the Jews because they "neither know me (Christ) nor my Father; if ye had known me, ye should have known my Father also."

The emphasis on fathers continues when Christ converses with some of his disciples about Abraham, the Jews' ancestral "father." Jesus asserts his word will make them "free," if they continue in it. They have, however, faith in their birth as a descendant of Abraham, and consider themselves already free. They are like Nicodemus, failing to understand the deeper meaning and claiming rights to the Kingdom of Heaven by virtue of their Hebraic ties to the Abrahamic covenant.

> They answered him, We be Abraham's seed, and were never in bondage to any man: how sayest thou, Ye shall be made free? (John 8:33)

Jesus answers that he came to free them from sin, referring to the true mission of the Messiah. "If the Son, therefore shall make you free, ye shall be free indeed." This freedom is true freedom because it is spiritual. "I speak that which

I have seen with my Father," Jesus testifies, " and
ye do that which ye have seen with your father."
The allusion is, of course, to Satan, their true
father, because they are "seeking to kill" Christ.
They are seeing through Satan's eyes. They are not
doing the works of Abraham, whom they claim as a
father. Furthermore, "Abraham rejoiced to see my
day and he saw it and was glad." They are not
seeing through Abraham's eyes. John wants to
bear testimony that the prophets of old such as
Abraham "saw" Christ's day and rejoiced. They
recognized him as the divine Son of the Father. If
the Jews really saw Abraham and were his
spiritual descendants then they would see Christ
and become "free" individuals through the coming
Atonement. "If God were your Father, ye would
love me for I proceeded forth and came from God,"
Jesus testifies. The Jews claimed both God and
Abraham as their fathers, but their rejection of
Christ is proof they never saw nor understood the
fathers they claimed, for to see God and the
prophets is to also see Jesus, the Son. To seek to kill
him is to see him as Satan saw him, i.e., a threat to
the establishment of his evil kingdom. John brings
this point out forcefully in the plots of the Sanhedrin
just prior to Christ's arrest. The leaders say:

> If we let him thus alone, all men
> will believe on him: and the Romans
> shall come and take away both our
> place and nation (John 11:48).

Their selfishness and desire for power are evident.

JOHN CHAPTER NINE
I Washed and I Received Sight

Chapter nine contains a marvelous example of John's theme of seeing. It is a capstone chapter which becomes a climax for this theme. It begins, as many earlier chapters, with a healing or miracle episode and then the subsequent discussion. In this case much of the discussion comes in chapter ten. In the beginning verses Christ heals a man born blind. Here is one who has never seen the light of day. Prior to giving him his sight Christ states once again his relationship to seeing. "I am the light of the world." We see because of Christ. He is the "spirit of truth," the source of all seeing, the supplier of all knowledge and wisdom. This truth is plainly taught in the 93rd section of the Doctrine and Covenants, which we will examine more closely later.

The blind man is sent to wash his eyes in the pool of Siloam. John tell us, "He went his way and washed and *came seeing*." What is it he sees? Certainly the light of day, the buildings and men, but he sees something more important which becomes apparent as the chapter proceeds.

He is questioned by the Pharisees and over and over again he testifies, "I went and washed and I *received sight*." There is a slight emphasis on washing and cleanliness in the young man's statements that may have significance also. He testifies later, "I washed and *do see*." The chapter continues with the futile attempts of the Pharisees to withstand or explain away the miracle, but the young man remains true and continues his testimony. All of this is evidence that he is no longer blind either physically or spiritually.

When the Pharisees accuse Christ of being a sinner in their own blindness the young man replies, "Whether he be a sinner or not, I know not; one thing I know, that whereas I was blind, *now I see.*" The Pharisees reject all his testimonies and "cast him out," or excommunicate him. Jesus then seeks him and asks him if he "believes on the Son of God." The young man asks the Savior to show him the Son of God, and he will believe. Christ replies, "Thou hast *seen* him." Both literally and spiritually the young man has seen Christ and he replies, "I believe." The more he sees of Christ, the stronger his belief will become. John has supplied us with another testimony, the testimony of one no longer blind.

Christ then pulls all the elements of chapter nine together. In doing so he restates John's theme and testimony. It is a challenge to the reader to overcome blindness in order to see, as the young man saw, "the Son of God," and in seeing, believe. John has placed this testimony in the center of his Gospel for it is central to his purpose. Many of the earlier sections culminate in this symbolic and literal chapter. Christ's own words at the conclusion of chapter nine bear testimony to its significance.

> And Jesus said, For judgment I am come into this world, that *they which see not might see* ; and that they which see might be made blind.

And some of the Pharisees
which were with him heard these
words, and said unto him, *Are we
blind also?"*
Jesus said unto them, If ye were
blind, ye should have no sin: but now
*ye say, We see; therefore your sin
remaineth* (John 9:39–41).

JOHN CHAPTER TEN
Therefore, Doth My Father Love Me

Chapter ten is a continuation of the dialogue
that started in chapter nine. It focuses on the
analogy of the Good Shepherd. In it we are given
the criteria for seeing true shepherds, (especially
the one true shepherd, Christ). The blind man has
heard the true Shepherd's voice and followed him.
All can know the true Shepherd, as the blind man
did, by understanding the love that will cause the
Good Shepherd to "lay down (his) life for the sheep."
Christ is testifying again that the true Messiah will
die. His death will be proof he is the Good
Shepherd. He will not run, leaving the sheep
defenseless as the "hireling" does, but will lay down
his life to save them from spiritual and physical
death. The disciples must see this truth in order to
continue to believe when the Savior is on the cross
and in the tomb. They must understand this love in
order to remain his disciples. John will soon teach
the necessity of shepherd–like love for those who
would be true disciples. The realization of Christ's
true mission and his love will create in each
disciple a much stronger faith, a faith even deeper

than the committing faith we saw evidenced in
Peter after the bread of life discourse given in
chapter six.

Christ follows his analogy of the Good
Shepherd with the relationship of himself to the
Father. This time John shows that the relation of
the Father and Son includes the commandment to
sacrifice his life for the sheep.

> Therefore doth my Father love
> me, because I lay down my life, that I
> might take it up again.
> No man taketh it from me, but I
> lay it down of myself. I have power to
> lay it down, and I have power to take it
> again. This commandment have I
> received of my Father (John 10:17–18).

As the Atonement is the most important
aspect of Christ's work, it is the single most
important truth a disciple must see. It is a key link
in the oneness of the Father and the Son. It is the
key link in the oneness of a disciple with Christ and
therefore with the Father. It is a oneness with the
Father created by the cleansing power of the
Atonement and the deep, grateful love it creates for
both the Father and Son.

The Jews are ready to stone Jesus with his
next major pronouncement: "I and my Father are
one." This is a culminating statement to all the
others Christ has made concerning his relationship with the Father. John's reporting of Christ's
earlier statements shows a foundation being laid
which bears this final pronouncement and

foreshadows it. Those earlier statements contain
the particulars of Christ's oneness with the Father.
He pleases the Father. He does what the Father
does and he speaks the Father's words. They are so
united in will and purpose and thought that the
"Father is in me and I am in him." Because of this
"oneness" Christ shall fulfill the Father's "will"
concerning the Atonement. The Father's will
becomes the Savior's will. After that "will" has
been fulfilled Christ can invite all his sheep to be
one with him as he is with the Father. Only his
Atonement can make this unity possible for "no
unclean thing can dwell with God" (1 Nephi 10:21).
Oneness is climaxed in the Intercessory Prayer of
chapter seventeen offered just prior to the agony of
Gethsemane. Carefully John is leading us to see
the one singular truth about Christ which will be
detailed with his death and resurrection.

We also see in the last verses of chapter ten
the same urgency spoken of earlier. The hour is
drawing near and they still do not accept him.

> If I do not the works of my
> Father, believe me not.
> But if I do, though ye believe not
> me, believe the works: that ye may
> know, and believe, that the Father is in
> me, and I in him (John 10:37–38).

JOHN CHAPTER ELEVEN
I Am the Resurrection and the Life

Chapter eleven contains the story of the
raising of Lazarus from the dead. All of the other

miracles have led up to this one. John places it in a central position in his Gospel. It is the culmination of all of Christ's earlier miracles, being the greatest, and it contains the promise of the greatest miracle he will yet accomplish, that of his resurrection and final victory over death.

An examination of all of Christ's miracles, particularly the healings, will reveal an underlying spiritual truth that will help us understand the meaning of the raising of Lazarus. Christ gave sight to the blind, hearing to the deaf. He raised the invalid that he might walk. He cleansed the leper and cast out devils. All of these whisper the promise of spiritual healing. Spiritually he came to give sight to the blind and hearing to those willing to listen. The spiritual cripple can walk and progress after his words. The unclean, outcast, spiritual lepers are cleansed and receive forgiveness through the Atonement. He cast out devils literally and figuratively. As the Atonement was accomplished he won a victory that will ultimately cast out Satan forever. With the raising of Lazarus Christ announces his victory over death in an ultimate sense. Not only would he raise Lazarus, dead for four days and buried, he would raise all men, calling them all to "come forth." He would do this by going into the realm of death itself. John places special emphasis on this chapter. Of all the miracles this is the most important because it is an outward sign of what John wants his readers most to see. Christ was not only a gentle teacher of righteousness and a healer, he was the conqueror of death and Satan.

John establishes this spiritual dimension
from the first. When Christ announces he will
return to Bethany upon hearing of Lazarus'
sickness, the apostles remind him of Jewish
attempts on his life. In his answer to them he
speaks of light and seeing.

> Jesus answered, Are there not
> twelve hours in the day? If any man
> walk in the day, he stumbleth not,
> because he seeth the light of this world.
> But if a man walk in the night,
> he stumbleth, because there is no light
> in him (John 11:9–10).

There is no need to fear for his safety as his
mission can only be accomplished in Jerusalem
with his death. But he will have the complete
"twelve hours" of his life to give light to men. If I
see the "light of this world" (Christ) I will not
stumble. If the apostles understand the necessity of
his death, they will not stumble either. Any
commitment will remain firm through an
understanding of his life and our own lives in
relation to his.

The disciples don't understand that Lazarus
is literally dead until Jesus, wanting no
misunderstanding, states plainly, "Lazarus is
dead." He then establishes the purpose of the
coming miracle.

> And I am glad for your sakes
> that I was not there, to the intent ye

may believe; nevertheless let us go unto
him (John 11:15).

What truth does Christ want the Apostles to
believe? Not only that he can bring a man back to
life. The Apostles already know this from
witnessing the raising of the son of the widow of
Nain and the daughter of Jairus. He wants them to
believe in his power over death in a much larger
sense. The Apostles must understand the power of
the Resurrection. Christ emphasizes his "intent"
to help them believe in his prayer at the grave of
Lazarus. He prays in gratitude to the Father for the
coming miracle "that they may believe that thou
hast sent me."

When the weeping Martha meets Christ
outside of Bethany the central message of chapter
eleven is plainly spoken. It is the spiritual truth
behind the outward miracle, and the central truth
of John's testimony. To see only the outward
miracle is to remain in darkness, to stumble, to see
the works of Christ, but not the Christ. In the story
of Lazarus, Jesus indicates to Martha the spiritual
understanding required of all who would be true
disciples.

> Jesus saith unto her, Thy
> brother shall rise again.
> Martha saith unto him, I know
> that he shall rise again in the
> resurrection at the last day.
> Jesus said unto her, *I am the*
> *resurrection, and the life: he that*

believeth in me, though he were dead,
yet shall he live:
And whosoever liveth and
believeth in me shall never die.
Believest thou this?
She saith unto him, Yea, Lord: I
believe that thou art the Christ, the Son
of God, which should come into the
world (John 11:23–27).

Martha's concluding testimony is one of
power. John never fails to include these
testimonies, for they enhance his purpose. In this
context Jesus is "the Christ, the Son of God"
because he will conquer death. The reiterated
testimonies all emphasize a belief in Christ and his
Atonement, even the one Christ's great enemy
Caiaphas will bear.
The rest of chapter eleven then details the
raising of Lazarus. After having the stone
removed, Christ "cried with a loud voice, Lazarus,
come forth."

And he that was dead came
forth, bound hand and foot with
graveclothes: and his face was bound
about with a napkin. Jesus saith unto
them. Loose him, and let him go (John
11:44).

We are then told that "many of the Jews
which came to see Mary, and had seen the things
which Jesus did, believed on him."

There is a pattern established in these last verses that will soon be repeated. As had Lazarus, so Christ himself will die and then be raised up. After his burial and the weeping of those women so close to him, the stone will be rolled away. He will *come forth*. His graveclothes and napkin will be removed, and many will then believe on him. The parallelism is evident. At that moment the disciples will begin to truly see their Lord and understand his glory, condescension, and mission.

This is the last miracle John relates. There is nothing left to teach symbolically. He can now proceed with the outward fulfillment of which the raising of Lazarus and all the other "signs" of Christ are but shadows of promise.

Let us now summarize what John has taught us. John has established through the miracles, stories and teachings of Christ as related in the first eleven chapters, several main truths about the Savior. These truths constitute John's testimony concerning the mission of the Savior. They center on changes and making things new. They are the great truths John wishes us to see. In summary we have learned that Christ brings cleansing and forgiveness of sins, new birth and progression. Christ reveals the Father's nature, character, attributes and perfections. Christ, as the light of the world and the Good Shepherd, brings understanding of the gospel's truths by opening eyes and unstopping ears, by offering the true bread and water to those who hunger and thirst. In that light true judgment can be rendered and forgiveness extended. And Christ brings life through his Resurrection and atoning sacrifice. If we have seen the Son of God in these aspects, true conversion can occur.

Chapter eleven concludes with the jealous plotting of the Pharisees and an allusion to the coming Passover. It serves as a prelude to the coming atoning sacrifice described in the following chapters. During their conversations, the high priest Caiaphas predicts the coming Atonement in the following words:

> Nor consider that it is expedient for us, that one man should die for the people, and that the whole nation perish not.
> And not for that nation only, but that also he should gather together in one the children of God that were scattered abroad (John 11:50,52).

John is very impressed with this prophecy. Although without true understanding, Christ's enemies bear witness to the necessity of his death. To emphasize this truth John adds a comment of his own.

> And this spake he not of himself: but being high priest that year, he prophesied that Jesus should die for that nation (John 11:51).

Once again a blindness is implied. Caiaphas does not see the significance of his own words. Nor does he realize that he will be the high priest who offers the real "Lamb of God" this Passover. This blindness, however, does not destroy the reality of his testimony. John is careful to record it for his readers.

John concludes chapter eleven with a reference to the coming Passover. He says, "...and many went out of the country up to Jerusalem before the Passover, *to purify* themselves." There is irony in this last statement. True purification comes through the Atonement. In very deed this Passover will purify the world. For those leaders, however, who precipitate this purification by condeming the Savior, the opposite will occur. In sacrificing Christ they spot their own garments with his blood and render themselves more impure than at any time in their lives.

JOHN CHAPTER TWELVE
We Would See Jesus

In chapter twelve we are once again taken to the home of Mary, Martha and Lazarus. Against the backdrop of the designing and murderous plots of the leaders, we view the devoted love of Mary as she anoints her beloved Master. This follows a pattern seen earlier in chapters three and four. We compared, at that time, Nicodemus, a leader, with the woman at the well. Now prior to Christ's sacrifice, the loving Mary anoints Christ's feet with costly oil and fills the house "with the odour of the ointment" in contrast to the evil plots of Christ's opponents. John's sensitive description of this scene indicates he was moved by the love of Mary. The complaint of Judas regarding the expense of

the oil prompts Jesus to give the following comfort
to Mary.

> Then said Jesus, Let her alone:
> for she hath preserved this ointment
> until now, that she might anoint me in
> token of my burial (JST John 12:7).

Joseph Smith has rendered a clearer
translation of this verse.   Mary apparently
perceives the coming storm and subsequent death.
She has sensed this death earlier and saved the
ointment for this moment. This is one of the first
indications that someone saw Christ's mission and
perhaps understood it before the Resurrection. We
are told immediately after this that "much
people...came not for Jesus' sake only, but that they
might see Lazarus also." The majority, by contrast
to Mary, came still seeing the miracles only, the
outward testimonies, not the inner truths those
testimonies represent.   Mary, however, understands and loves on a deeper level. We can also
contrast Mary's open anointing of Christ in the face
of criticism prior to his Atonement, with
Nicodemus and Joseph of Arimathaea's anointing
of Christ after his death. They did it "secretly for
fear of the Jews" (John 19:38–40).
The believers in outward miracles,
impressed with the spectacular raising of Lazarus,
welcome Christ triumphantly to Jerusalem in the
next verses.   John specifically tells us that the
multitude came for Lazarus' sake.

"For this cause the people also
met him, for that they heard that he
had done this miracle (John 12:18).

However, the people, and even the Apostles,
don't realize, Christ's triumph will be a triumph
over death, won by his own death. It will be a
triumph over sin, won through suffering. In truth
their King has come to them, but he comes in
humility on a donkey, not a war horse. He will
conquer sin and Satan, not Romans or Greeks. His
conquest will be for all mankind: Jew, Samaritan,
and Gentile.

As if to emphasize this point, John relates
the story of "certain Greeks" who approach Philip
(a Greek name) and say, "Sir, we would *see* Jesus."
Jesus responds by conversing with the Greeks.
Jesus teaches them that if they would truly "*see
him*" they must see his coming death. Jesus'
teaching during this conversation explains his
coming "triumph," and provides a deeper answer
to the Greeks desire, "We would *see* Jesus." Christ
immediately tells the Greeks, "The hour is come
that the Son of man should be glorified." He
explains the method of that glorification with an
analogy that would have significant meaning to
Greeks. The analogy he uses is the planting and
harvesting of corn or wheat. Considering that one
of the most important Greek myths revolved around
Demeter the Goddess of Corn and her daughter
Persephone's annual return to the underworld,
this analogy would in all probability be understood
by one coming from a Greek background. Christ's
analogy is given as follows:

> Verily, verily, I say unto you,
> Except a corn of wheat fall into the
> ground and die, it abideth alone: but if
> it die, it bringeth forth much fruit.
> He that loveth his life shall lose
> it; and he that hateth his life in this
> world shall keep it unto life eternal
> (John 12:24–25).

If the Greeks are to "see" or understand Jesus as the true Messiah they must understand that he is the "corn of wheat" that will fall into the ground and die. They will be part of the "much fruit" that his death will produce by the power of the Resurrection.

These words are followed by a very poignant prayer offered by the Savior to his Father. During this prayer we are allowed a glimpse into the soul of Christ as he contemplates the coming Atonement. It requires no commentary.

> Now is my soul troubled; and
> what shall I say? Father, save me
> from this hour: but for this cause
> came I unto this hour.
> Father, glorify thy name. Then
> came there a voice from heaven,
> saying, I have both glorified it, and will
> glorify it again (John 12:27–28).

Some in the crowd, evidently lacking in neccessary faith heard thunder and not the Father's voice.

John is the only writer who relates this testimony of the Father. It is significant, in light of

the overarching power of the Atonement, that it
was heard by "certain Greeks that came up to
worship at the feast." John has taught earlier that
the Atonement covers all mankind who accept
Christ, not just the covenant seed of Abraham.
These Greeks are worthy to hear the testimony of
the Father. Christ, speaking to those who heard
the voice, explains that it "came...for your sakes."
In other words, to help them believe.

How will God glorify Christ's name? The
answer comes immediately from the lips of the
Savior as he predicts the coming crucifixion.

> Now is the judgment of this
> world: now shall the prince of this
> world be cast out.
> And I, if I be lifted up from the
> earth, will draw all men unto me"
> (John 12:31–32).

There is double meaning in this
pronouncement. The world is about to judge
Christ. The judgment will be based on appearance,
not truth. The world will condemn its own "light."
This judgment is referred to in Nephi's vision when
he contemplates the spacious building of his
father's dream. The angel commenting on this
crucifixion of Christ tells Nephi with an ironic and
perhaps sarcastic tone of sorrow, "Behold, the
world and the wisdom thereof" (1 Nephi 11:33). On
the other hand, the world is about *to be judged*
because of its crucifixion of Christ. This too will be
a judgment of condemnation, but God will be the
judge and his condemnation of the world for the

death of his Son will be just. There is a third implication seen in these simple words. In another sense Christ has judged the world or mankind worthy of his Atonement. He will allow himself to be cast out in order to bring salvation to all who will accept him.

The double meaning continues in the next phrase. Christ, as the Firstborn Son, is literally the "prince of this world." He is about to be cast out by his coming death. However, "the prince of this world" is also used to designate the devil. The casting out of the true prince, Christ, will overcome the power of the false prince, Satan, and cast him out of the life of every repentant soul. Eventually Christ will cast him into darkness forever.

There is also double meaning in the second sentence Christ utters. "And I, if I be lifted up from the earth, will draw all men unto me" (John 12:32).

Being "lifted up" refers to the crucifixion. He will be "lifted up" upon the cross. It can also refer to being lifted up or raised from the grave through the power of the Atonement and his Resurrection. This second lifting will have the power to "draw all men" unto Christ, both through the cleansing power of his sacrifice and his resurrection. Understanding the pain and anguish of Christ's Atonement and his love for humanity will naturally "draw" men to him. How can one not love and come to the Savior, a shepherd who will "lay down (his) life for the sheep?"

As we have seen so many times before, the people fail to understand. Their tradition stands in their way. "We have heard that Christ abideth

forever" they answer, "and how sayest thou the Son
of man must be lifted up?" They have caught the
meaning of the phrase "lifted up", but not the
Resurrection and Atonement nor the necessity of
that lifting up."

They believe the true Messiah will not die.
Their statement is also filled with irony. Christ
will in truth "abide forever," but only through his
death and promised resurrection.

Christ responds to their question and
unbelief with a reference to seeing and light. They
are still in darkness and his light is soon to be taken
to Calvary. His tone must have been one of
sorrowful resignation for their continued
blindness.

> Then Jesus said unto them, Yet
> a little while is the light with you.
> Walk while ye have the light, lest
> darkness come upon you: for he that
> walketh in darkness knoweth not
> whither he goeth.
> While ye have light, believe in
> the light, that ye may be the children of
> light... (John 12:35–36).

The emphasis is on knowing "whither he
goeth." Earlier in chapter eight Christ testified, "I
know whence I came and whither I go." The
promise is now extended that all who walk in his
light will know not only where Christ "goeth," but
where they too can follow. This will find fulfillment
in the Last Supper's teachings on Christ's many
mansions. We would add that those who walk in

the light will also know from "whence (they) came."
John concludes chapter twelve with his own
comments. He summarizes with the verb and idea
that he commenced with—that of seeing. We are
told, "Though he had done so many miracles before
them, yet they believed not on him." In John's
mind this fulfills a prophecy made by Isaiah which
he then quotes.

> ...Lord who hath believed our
> report? and to whom hath the arm of
> the Lord been revealed?
> He hath blinded their eyes, and
> hardened their heart; that they should
> not see with their eyes, nor understand
> with their heart, and be converted, and
> I should heal them.
> These things said Esaias, when
> he saw his glory, and spake of him
> (John 12:38, 40–41).

The emphasis is still on seeing. The first
quote from Isaiah comes from chapter fifty–three.
In that chapter the meekness, death and
Atonement of Christ is described. Isaiah saw
Christ truly and realized that others would not
believe in a Messiah of meekness, a Savior who
dies. They would not understand the "arm of the
Lord" or how God's strength would be revealed in
his Son's death. They would be blind and their
blindness would prevent their conversion and
subsequent healing. Isaiah is now added to Moses
and Abraham as a prophet quoted by John or
Christ, who saw and accepted the Son of God.

John continues his commentary on Isaiah by an explanation of the prophecied blindness. "For they loved the praise of men more than the praise of God." This is once again reminiscent of Nicodemus' conversation with Christ and the warning he received concerning evil deeds and darkness. John then continues the narrative with a pronouncement of Christ's that stresses the urgency felt by the Savior, the lack of sight evidenced by the people, and the relationship he enjoyed with his Father.

> Jesus cried and said, He that believeth on me, believeth not on me, but on him that sent me.
>
> And he that seeth me seeth him that sent me.
>
> I am come a light into the world, that whosoever believeth on me should not abide in darkness.
>
> And if any man hear my words, and believe not, I judge him not: for I came not to judge the world, but to save the world (John 12: 44–47).

The judgment of the world was spoken of earlier. The world has judged itself by its condemnation of Christ. The world has judged Christ unworthy and condemns him to death. However, the Son judges the world worthy of saving even at the price of his own suffering and death. In three verses Christ has detailed much that John has focused on throughout his testimony. If we see Christ we will see the Father. If we don't, we will

live in spiritual darkness. We must see that Christ
didn't come to "judge" the world meaning
"condemn" the world. He came to save the world.
These phrases echo his words to Nicodemus once
again. There is additional irony in these words.
Christ, the true judge of the world is about to be
judged by the world and found guilty of the one
crime he could not possibly commit, that of
blasphemy—for he was in truth the Son of God, the
Messiah.

This concludes the first half of John's
Gospel. He has attempted to show us that all of
Christ's life and everything he did pointed to the
atoning sacrifice, his true mission. He has also
shown the relationship of the Son to the Father.
The second half now revolves around the last hours
of his mortal life and the morning of his
resurrection. It will focus on a new theme, love
and sacrifice, which will be given emphasis at the
Last Supper.

CHAPTER THREE

To See By the Light of Love

JOHN CHAPTER THIRTEEN
He Loved Them Unto the End

In the second half of his Testimony, John continues to work with seeing and the Father/Son relationship. He also introduces a new theme, one that dominates the last half of John's Gospel and also his Epistles. This theme is love or charity. We have sensed Christ's love in the first half, especially in those moments of urgency when Christ "cries" for the people to accept, be converted and healed. We see it in the tender forgiveness of sins, the quiet moments of healing, his weeping at the tomb of Lazarus, and in his parable of the Good Shepherd. Its full power is taught in the Last Supper and lived in the Atonement. In the Last Supper Christ speaks of love. This love is what John wishes us now to see more fully for it is a key to our becoming one with Christ and his Father. In the Garden and on the cross he fully demonstrates his charity, thus giving us a perfect example of all he taught.

As if to signal to his readers this new emphasis on Christ, John introduces the last hours of the Savior's life with a statement of the Savior's love.

> Now before the feast of the passover, when Jesus knew that his hour was come that he should depart out of this world unto the Father, having loved his own which were in the world, he loved them unto the end (John 13:1).

This testimony is followed by an example of Christ's love—that of the washing of the disciples' feet. The type of love Christ demonstrates and demands is the love of service, meekness, and humility. The Apostles had been quarreling again over who was greatest. The washing of their feet is the answer to that quarrel; he who is greatest is the servant of all—the one least concerned with his own greatness.

When Peter refuses to let Jesus wash him he is told, "What I do thou knowest not now, but thou shalt know hereafter." There is much implied in this statement. Part of the implication can be found in the meaning of the ordinance of washing of feet discussed in section eighty–eight of the Doctrine and Covenants. However, there is also a promise that Peter will come to understand the type of love that would cause the "Son of Man" to wash his brother's feet. In order that there will be no

misunderstanding, Christ forcefully brings home
the message.

> Ye call me Master and Lord:
> and ye say well; for so I am.
> If I then, your Lord and Master,
> have washed your feet; ye also ought to
> wash one another's feet.
> For I have given you an
> example, that ye should do as I have
> done to you.
> If ye know these things, happy
> are ye if you do them (John 13:13–15,
> 17).

Christ has exemplified the highest order of
humility. The deepest humility is not seen when a
person of an obviously lesser station acknowledges
someone of greater nobility. Deep humility is
evidenced when a being of higher station
condescends with love to serve those of a lower
station. In this case the Master washes the
servant, in a picture of true humility. With the
description of this act of Christ, John has set the
stage for the commandment to love each other with
true humility. He has shown us the perfect
example of it.

John returns to the "seeing" theme a few
verses later. Christ tells the Apostles that he will be
betrayed. This betrayal will eventually lead to his
death. Because the Apostles do not yet fully
understand or see the true mission of Christ, he
does not want them to lose faith in him when his
death is an accomplished fact. Therefore he says:

Now I tell you before it come,
that, when it is come to pass, ye may
believe that I am the Christ (JST John
13:19).

This is followed by the giving of a "sop" to
Judas who leaves the supper to complete the
betrayal. John then states, with obvious undertones
to light and darkness, (repeated symbols in the
Gospel that enhance the theme of sight), "...and it
was night." Not only is it night literally, but the evil
deeds spoken of by Christ in his conversation with
Nicodemus are about to be done in the darkness of
the night. This eases the tension and atmosphere
in the room and Jesus immediately proclaims his
coming glorification through the Atonement which
Judas' betrayal will precipitate. John then returns
to the main thrust of the Last Supper—that of love
by giving us the Savior's words.

A new commandment I give
unto you, That ye love one another; as I
have loved you, that ye also love one
another.
By this shall all men know that
ye are my disciples, if ye have love one
to another (John 13:34–35).

In an all encompassing commandment we
have been introduced to a major aspect of
conversion and testimony. Christ's disciples will be
known by the love they bear to one another. In the
following chapters this new emphasis will be seen
again and again, as it will be seen in the First

Epistle. This love will give the disciples the desire
to "wash one another's feet" as Jesus commanded
them to do.

Jesus has told the Apostles that where he is
going, they cannot follow. It is at this moment that
Luke tells us Jesus turned to Peter and said:

> Simon, Simon, behold, Satan
> hath desired you, that he may sift the
> children of the kingdom as wheat:
> But I have prayed for thee, that
> thy faith fail not: and when thou art
> converted strengthen thy brethren (JST
> Luke 22:31–32).

It is significant that Christ would use the
word "converted." Peter feels he is converted. We
have seen in John six that his conversion has
reached the stage of commitment. Peter assures
the Savior, "I will lay down my life for thy sake."
Christ follows with the prophesy of Peter's three
denials. It is interesting to note that Peter uses the
same words Christ used when referring to his
Atonement. There is only one difference. Peter's
love for the Savior is not yet as fully developed as
Christ's love for Peter. In the moment of pain,
Christ's love would not fail him and he would "lay
down" his life. As for Peter there would come three
denials. He was not yet fully "converted," yet we
should not judge nor condemn Peter. The day
would come when his conversion would cause him
to "lay down (his) life for (the Savior's) sake." At
this stage of Peter's life the Savior does not want his

death, for on Peter's shoulders would rest the weight of the early church in the coming years.

What did Peter lack in his being "converted"? As has been indicated throughout John's testimony, the Apostles did not see the true mission of Christ in its fulness. They did not understand all the reasons for his coming death and Atonement. Full realization would come with the Resurrection and the gift of the Holy Ghost. This seeing is necessary for a deep and abiding conversion.

The disciples lack this depth of vision. They did not understand nor possess at this time the love for each other and the "sheep of his fold" that Christ urges them to develop during the Last Supper. By contrast, Christ truly sees his mission and deeply loves, enough to "lay down" his life.

These two qualities, *comprehensive vision* and the *love that arises from deep humility*, more than anything else, constitute lasting conversion. They mark a true disciple, because they are Christlike. In the first half of his Gospel, John tried to help his readers obtain comprehensive sight. In the second half he will try to help us develop Christlike love, for that love is part of a total vision of the Master and his Father.

JOHN CHAPTER FOURTEEN
Shew Us the Father

Chapter fourteen begins with one of the most beautiful statements made by Christ. It is a continuation of the theme of love introduced in chapter thirteen.

Let not your heart be troubled: ye
believe in God, believe also in me.

In my Father's house are many
mansions: if it were not so, I would
have told you. I go to prepare a place
for you.

And if I go and prepare a place
for you, I will come again, and receive
you unto myself; that where I am,
there ye may be also (John 14:1–3).

This pronouncement is followed by Christ's
statement that he is "the way, the truth and the
life." The mansions are the destination of all men.
Christ is the road that leads to them. John will
teach us that road by showing us what main aspect
of Christ's life we must follow to inherit "a
mansion" in the Father's house. It will not be
surprising to anyone that love plays an important
part in that road—both the love of Christ (who will
atone, that he might become "the way") and the love
we must have for each other in order to follow him.
This scripture is also given as a comfort to
the Apostles who are troubled by Christ's
declaration concerning his coming death. Herein
we have an example of Christ's selfless love. Let us
examine it.

What does the Savior know as he partakes of
the Last Supper with his Apostles? He knows that
Judas at that moment is betraying him. He knows
that Peter will deny him three times. He knows the
other Apostles will "be scattered, every man to his
own, and shall leave me alone." He knows that
within hours the weight of the world's sins will be

placed upon him in Gethsemane. He knows he will be mocked, beaten, spit upon, and finally crucified. If ever, in the history of the world, there was a man who needed words of comfort, love and support, it was the Savior at this time. But he looked upon the troubled faces of those he loved, and gave comfort instead of receiving it. This is true and selfless love and a great example to all mankind. We see the Savior's humility once more. Over and over again in the following chapters we will read Christ's comforting words. He told the Apostles not to be troubled, yet days earlier he said to the Greeks who came to see him, "Now is my soul troubled." In spite of the weight he bears, his focus is still on other's needs and fears. Later in chapter fourteen Christ repeats his consolation with the following beautiful promise.

> Peace I leave with you, my peace I give unto you: not as the world giveth, give I unto you. Let not your heart be troubled, neither let it be afraid.
> Ye have heard how I said unto you, I go away, and come again unto you. If ye loved me, ye would rejoice, because I said, I go unto the Father: for my Father is greater than I (John 14:27–28).

Christ teaches the Apostles that if they had the kind of selfless love he possesses, they would rejoice in his death knowing he returns to his

Father. Again we see the emphasis on others. He who needed comfort is the comforter.

In chapter fourteen Jesus teaches the Apostles the true evidence of a man's love for Christ. "If ye love me keep my commandments." True love then can be shown by the Apostles in three ways. One—they must "love one another." Two—they must have a selfless love which will cause them to rejoice at Christ's return to his Father. The major part of this rejoicing will come with the realization of the blessings for *all the world* that will result from the Son's return to his Father, and Three—they must keep his commandments. There is a beautiful promise then given to those who truly love in these ways.

> ...If a man love me, he will keep my words: and my Father will love him, and we will come unto him, and make our abode with him" (John 14:23).

John has brought us back to the theme of the Father/Son relationship and linked it with love. He has told us of Christ's invitation to all to become one with the Father as he is one with the Father. Love, in the above three ways, will bring the Father and Son intimately into a man's life. This invitation and promise will reach its fruition in the spoken Intercessory Prayer of Christ in chapter seventeen prior to the prayer of agony in Gethsemane. It will reach its literal fruition in the Savior's Atonement and Resurrection. Only through Christ's Atonement and Resurrection, the sign of his love, can the

Father and Son's permanent "abode" be shared with men. This is the meaning of Christ's earlier statement made to Thomas.

> ...I am the way, the truth, and the life: no man cometh unto the Father, but by me (John 14:6).

The love of Christ will be further manifested to the Apostles through the gift of the Holy Ghost which Christ promises to send as a "Comforter." When he comes he will "teach you all things and bring all things to your remembrance." Again the emphasis is on the Apostles need of comfort, not Christ's . The promise of the Holy Ghost is followed by another promise.

> I will not leave you comfortless: I will come to you.
> Yet a little while, and the world seeth me no more; but ye see me: because I live, ye shall live also (John 14:18–19).

John has brought us back to the "seeing" theme. The statement implies once again that the world does not see the Savior. Because the world did not see him in life they will "see him no more," both literally and figuratively after his death. Their blindness will cause them to fight the Apostles and their testimonies until the whole world plunges into apostasy. The Apostles, however "see" Jesus as the Messiah and in the coming days they will understand even more as they become special

witnesses of his Resurrection. They will be invited
at that time to "handle (him) and see" (Luke 24:39).
Their seeing and loving will bring them eternal life.

There remains one last theme to respond to
in chapter fourteen, that of the Father/Son
relationship and its connection with "seeing." It
comes early in the conversation with the Apostles.
Jesus reiterates his earlier teachings—that to know
Christ is to know the Father. It will be remembered
that one of the missions of Christ that John wishes
to stress is Christ's ability through his life and
teachings to reveal to humanity the nature of the
Father. At the Last Supper Jesus tells the Apostles:

> If ye had known me, ye should
> have known my Father also: and from
> henceforth ye know him, and have
> seen him (John 14:7).

To see Christ is to know the Father. This
statement draws from Philip a request. "...Shew us
the Father, and it sufficeth us."

The answer Philip receives indicates that he,
(and in all probability the other Apostles), did not
fully understood this element of Jesus' mission.
John wants all to understand it.

> Jesus saith unto him, Have I
> been so long time with you, and yet
> hast thou not known me, Philip? he
> that hath seen me hath seen the
> Father; and how sayest thou then,
> Shew us the Father?

> Believest thou not that I am in
> the Father, and the Father in me?
> (John 14:9–10)

This is the culmination statement of the
Father/Son theme as it relates to a comprehensive
vision of the ministry of Christ. It is sad that so
many sincere Christian people still do not
understand this aspect of John's testimony and
quote the above scripture in support of their own
creeds. Those creeds claim Christ and the Father
are one in essence, in a mystical, literal unity. But
if one reads John carefully, looking at this theme as
it is treated throughout the Gospel, it becomes
obvious the desired unity and oneness is not as the
Christian creeds teach, but one of work, will,
personality, perfections, character and words. In
this sense we see the Father when we see the Son.

The chapter ends with the Savior's repeated
statement that he is telling them of his death before
it is accomplished that "ye might believe." He then
prepares to go to Gethsemane and the Atonement.
Christ's final words at the Last Supper, as
rendered by Joseph Smith, show once again the
pure nature of the Savior's love.

> Hereafter I will not talk much
> with you: for the prince of darkness,
> who is of this world, cometh, but hath
> no power over me, *but he hath power
> over you.*
> But that the world may know
> that *I love the Father*; and as *the
> Father gave me commandment*, even

so I do. Arise, let us go hence (JST
John 14:30–31).

The Prince of Light tells his Apostles that he
is willing to atone, to cast out the "prince of
darkness" for two reasons, both center on love and
bear testimony that Christ exhibits the same type of
love he demands. The Apostles were told to: (1.)
love each other; and, (2.) to keep the
commandments if they loved Christ. Christ
teaches in the above verses that: (1.) He will atone
(an evidence of his love for them), because the devil
"hath power over you." He does this that they
might break free of Satan's power as he is free of it;
and, (2.) he will show "that I love the Father" by
keeping the commandment of the Father, the
command to atone. He will not require of his
disciples anything that he is not willing to perform.
After teaching this by word, Christ is ready to teach
it by deed and he therefore says, "Arise, let us go
hence."

JOHN CHAPTER FIFTEEN
Ye Are My Friends

Chapters fifteen and sixteen contain the
teachings of Christ as he walks with his Apostles to
Gethsemane, or perhaps they were taught by or in
the Garden. All of the themes introduced in
chapters thirteen and fourteen are emphasized.
The Savior begins with an analogy of a vine. In
chapter fourteen Christ taught that he was in the
Father and the Father in him. In the analogy an
invitation is given to the apostles to share this same

unity with Christ and therefore with the Father.
He tells the Apostles:

> Abide in me, and I in you. As
> the branch cannot bear fruit of itself,
> except it abide in the vine; no more can
> ye, except ye abide in me (John 15:4).

This unity is stressed further when the
analogy is over and the Savior is commenting on it.
His commentary centers around love once again for
only in love is a true unity achieved. "As the Father
hath loved me, so have I loved you: continue ye in
my love" (John 15:9).
How does one continue in Christ's love? The
answer is given immediately, re–emphasizing the
need to keep commandments.

> If ye keep my commandments,
> ye shall abide in my love; even as I
> have kept my Father's command-
> ments, and abide in his love (John
> 15:10).

Christ uses himself as the example of true
love by repeating the words he said just prior to
leaving the Last Supper. He is keeping his Father's
commandment. By keeping that commandment he
shows his love for his Father and receives the
Father's love in return. This is the relationship
Christ wishes to share with the disciples. In the
Intercessory Prayer of chapter seventeen it is
expanded to include all who believe in him (John
17:20–21).

To further specify the depth of this love,
Christ once again uses himself as an example. He
shows his love in the fullest depth and sense by
obeying the commandment to atone, but he also
shows it to his disciples by pronouncing them his
"friends." He wants them to love each other as
friends in the same manner that he loves them.

> This is my commandment, That
> ye love one another, as I have loved
> you.
> Greater love hath no man than
> this, that a man lay down his life for
> his friends.
> Ye are my friends, if ye do
> whatsoever I command you (John
> 15:12–14).

The commandment given by the Father to the
Savior involved the salvation of his children. The
commandment given by the Savior to the Apostles
will involve the salvation of his Father's children
also. "I have chosen you, and ordained you that ye
should go and bring forth fruit..." Christ tells the
disciples. In other words, they will also show their
love for the Savior and his Father by working for the
salvation of souls. Because they will do this, Christ
can call them his "friends" instead of servants.
"The servant knoweth not what his Lord doth,"
Christ teaches. The "friends" share the same
desire, will, and goals, of the Savior. They see his
work and desire to do that same work. The one who
works for the salvation of his fellowman as Christ
did, becomes the friend of Christ. He becomes one

with him and one with the Father by uniting with
them in their eternal purpose. This is important
for the Apostles to see as they will soon be given the
responsibility to take the gospel to "every creature"
(Mark 16:15).

However, if one does the work of Christ and
becomes his "friend," the world will treat the friend
as he did the Master. Christ warns the Apostles,
therefore, that they will be "hated" by the world.

> If the world hate you, ye know
> that it hated me before it hated you.
> If ye were of the world, the world
> would love his own: but because ye are
> not of the world, but I have chosen you
> out of the world, therefore the world
> hateth you (John 15:18–19).

The "friend" should not expect better
treatment than the Master if he does the Master's
work. Continuing with the unity and oneness
theme he has established, Christ teaches that those
who hate him, also hate the Father.

> He that hateth me hateth my
> father also.
> ...but now have they both *seen*
> and hated both me and my Father
> (John 15:23–24).

The use of the verb "to see" is once again
paradoxical and ironic. In truth they have not seen
the Savior or his Father. However, because of the
oneness of Christ and his Father they have seen

and hated the Father by hating Christ. In this way
they have seen the Father and also rejected him.
The Apostles will also be hated in this way. The
world's hatred of the Apostles will be proof of the
Apostles oneness with Christ and the Father.

JOHN CHAPTER SIXTEEN
A Little While and Ye Shall See Me

Chapter sixteen returns us to the comforting
love of Christ for his disciples. He is now moments
away from entering the garden to atone. His words
continue to be words of comfort.

> But now I go my way to him that
> sent me; and none of you asketh me,
> Whither goest thou?
> But because I have said these
> things unto you, sorrow hath filled
> your heart.
> Nevertheless I tell you the truth;
> It is expedient for you that I go
> away...(John 16:5–7).

The focus is still on the Apostles' needs.
Christ promises them the comforter again and tells
them that the Holy Ghost will teach them all the
things they "cannot bear now." The Holy Ghost will
also help them to see by "shewing them things to
come. He shall glorify me; for he shall receive of
mine, and shall shew it unto you." The Holy Ghost
will be a key factor in their seeing all
things—including the Savior. This promise is
followed by the last pronouncement of the Savior

regarding seeing.   It is a critical one for
understanding the total usage of this verb
throughout John. It is a capstone statement to the
others, and goes hand in hand with the Isaiah
quotes given in chapter twelve. It is also a leading
statement concerning the coming Atonement for
sin and the conquest of death through the
Resurrection. The emphasis and space John gives
it indicates it is important to his overall purpose.

> A little while, and ye shall not
> see me: and again, a little while, and
> ye shall see me, because I go to the
> Father (John 16:16).

The Apostles do not understand this
statement and discuss its meaning among
themselves. They come to no conclusion saying,
"We cannot tell what he saith." Jesus responds to
their desire to ask its meaning by repeating his
statement, "Do ye enquire among yourselves of that
I said; A little while, and ye shall not see me: and
again, a little while, and ye shall see me?" This
time we need not interpret the meaning of Christ's
words for ourselves. Jesus supplies the meaning.
His explanation contains the promise that the
Apostles will finally truly see the Christ. However,
it will take the Resurrection and the Holy Ghost for
a comprehensive vision of the Savior to find
fulfillment. The explanation by Christ is given as
follows:

> Verily, verily, I say unto you,
> That ye shall weep and lament, but the

> world shall rejoice: and ye shall be
> sorrowful, but your sorrow shall be
> turned into joy.
>
> A woman when she is in travail
> hath sorrow, because her hour is
> come: but as soon as she is delivered of
> the child, she remembereth no more
> the anguish, for joy that a man is born
> into the world.
>
> And ye now therefore have
> sorrow: but I will see you again, and
> your heart shall rejoice, and your joy
> no man taketh from you (John
> 16:20–22).

The Apostles will weep at Christ's death
because they will not see him anymore, but that
sorrow will turn to joy when they see his
resurrected body and understand his mission and
its implication for themselves and mankind. This
denotes both a physical and spiritual vision. The
promise is given to all who see the Savior, his true
role, of a "joy" that can never be taken away. This
is the blessing of conversion. John would have all
men receive this joy.

This promise is followed by another. Earlier,
Philip asked Jesus to show him the Father,
indicating a lack of understanding and a failure to
perceive part of Christ's mission. Now, moments
before the Atonement will begin, Jesus tells the
Apostles:

> These things have I spoken unto
> you in proverbs: but the time cometh,

when I shall no more speak unto you
in proverbs, but I shall shew you
plainly of the Father (John 16:25).

How will Christ show them plainly of the
Father? The answer comes in several ways.
One—after the Resurrection they will literally see a
glorified celestial resurrected being as is the
Father. Two—they will comprehend the Father's
love in sending his "Only Begotten Son that
whosoever believeth in him should not perish but
have everlasting life." They will comprehend their
own need to develop that same type of love.
Three—they will also see that through the
Atonement they can be one with the Father and the
Son by becoming celestial, glorified resurrected
beings, true "friends" sharing the same
aspirations, goals, wills and characters, reflecting
back to the Savior his own divine light. Their
preaching of the gospel "in all the world" will be
proof of their friendship.

This love of the Father for the disciples is
further pointed to in verse twenty–seven. "For the
Father himself loveth you, because ye have loved
me, and have believed that I came out from God."
To feel this love helps one to understand the Father.

The Apostles assure Jesus that they now
understand and believe, but Jesus knows they will
not really see and understand until after the
Resurrection and the reception of the Holy Ghost.
He responds to their statements of belief with a
question, a prophesy, and a final word of comfort.

...Do ye now believe?
Behold, the hour cometh, yea, is
now come, that ye shall be scattered,
every man to his own, and shall leave
me alone: and yet I am not alone,
because the Father is with me.
These things I have spoken unto
you, that in me ye might have peace.
In the world ye shall have tribulation:
but be of good cheer; I have overcome
the world (John 16:31–33).

Christ's love overcame the world. That love
will now accomplish the Atonement. The Apostles
love will lead them to overcome the world also.

JOHN CHAPTER SEVENTEEN
That They May Be One In Us

This brings us to the great Intercessory
Prayer of chapter seventeen. Christ is now
moments away from the beginning of the
Atonement. We see in these last moments with his
Apostles the final example of selfless love. Even in
these moments when Matthew tells us he "began to
be sorrowful and very heavy," (Matthew 26:37) he is
concerned with others. He kneels and prays,not for
himself, but for the disciples and all who will
believe.

I pray for them: I pray not for
the world, but for them which thou
hast given me; for they are thine.

And all mine are thine, and
thine are mine; and I am glorified in
them.
And now I am no more in the
world, but these are in the world, and I
come to thee. Holy Father, keep
through thine own name those whom
thou hast given me, that they may be
one, as we are (John 17:9–11).

This prayer is the culmination of the
invitation to be one with Christ as he is with the
Father. If we are one with Christ we will also be
one with the Father. In this prayer we find a fuller
meaning to the description of Zion, a place where
people are of "one heart and one mind." Certainly
Zion is a place of total unity with one's brothers and
sisters. However, chapter seventeen indicates that
one heart and one mind is also a unity with Christ
and the Father. This John fully understood as is
evidenced in all his writings. A truly converted
individual will seek and maintain a oneness with
both the Godhead and his fellowman Only in this
manner can a true Zion society be formed and
maintained. Only in this manner can we obey the
two great commandments of the law that we love
God with all our hearts and our neighbor as
ourself.
In the prayer we also find this all inclusive
statement:

And this is life eternal, that they
might know thee the only true God,

and Jesus Christ, whom thou hast
sent" (John 17:3).

We can now understand a fuller meaning to
this oft quoted scripture. John's whole Gospel has
been teaching us the way to "know the only true
God." We know God by knowing his Son and being
one with them and with each other through the
Atonement and the binding power of love, a love of
deepest humility.

The prayer is beautiful in its depth of love and
its simplicity of desire. It needs very little
commentary. Notice how so many of John's
themes are intertwined, blended and given life by
the prayer of Christ.

I pray not that thou shouldest
take them out of the world, but that
thou shouldest keep them from the evil.

They are not of the world, even
as I am not of the world.

Sanctify them through thy truth:
thy word is truth.

As thou hast sent me into the
world, even so have I also sent them
into the world.

And for their sakes I sanctify
myself, that they also might be
sanctified through the truth.

Neither pray I for these alone,
but for them also which shall believe on
me through their word;

That they all may be one; as
thou, Father, art in me, and I in thee,

that they also may be one in us: that
the world may believe that thou hast
sent me.

And the glory which thou gavest
me I have given them; that they may be
one, even as we are one:

I in them, and thou in me, that
they may be made perfect in one; and
that the world may know that thou hast
sent me, and hast loved them, as thou
hast loved me (John 17:15–23).

John makes no commentary on Christ's
prayer. He simply reports it, knowing it would
stand on its own. It is one of the climaxes of John's
Gospel. In it we find a deep intensity. Christ
desires a unity among his disciples "that the world
may know that thou hast sent me." One might
pause at this moment, and ponder. Has the
Christian world heeded the Savior's most fervent
prayer?

With this prayer recorded, John's purposes
have largely been fulfilled. What remains is the
testimony that Christ actually accomplished all he
had promised to do during his ministry. The final
four chapters are therefore mostly narrative. They
relate the actual events of the final hours up to and
including the Resurrection. Chapters eighteen and
nineteen tell of the trial and death. Twenty tells of
the Resurrection and twenty–one contains an
exhortation in the form of an epilogue. These final
chapters maintain a thematic balance we have seen
dominating John's Gospel, that of seeing, light,
love, and the Father/Son relationship.

JOHN CHAPTER EIGHTEEN
I Find in Him No Fault At All

Chapter eighteen begins with the arrest.
John alone of all the other Gospels tells us of the
conversation prior to Christ being taken to the
various trials.   John, wanting to stress the
willingness of Christ to drink "the cup which my
Father hath given me," states:

> Jesus...knowing all things that
> should come upon him, went forth,
> and said unto them, (those who came
> to take him), *Whom seek ye*? (John
> 18:4)

There is no hesitancy on the part of Christ.
He "went forth." The words "whom seek ye" are
very powerful. They serve as a reminder to all of
us.   Each man must ask this question of
himself—whom do I seek? The first words Christ
spoke to John on the day John the Baptist testified to
him and Andrew were, "What seek ye?" We now
hear the question repeated.   Once again, a
wholeness and unity is seen in John's Gospel.
Christ is told by the arresting officers that
they seek "Jesus of Nazareth." Christ answers this
response with another statement that holds power.
It is a testimony and an answer. "*I am he*," Jesus
declares. He is more than Jesus of Nazareth. He is
the one whom all men should seek. We hear Christ
testifying of himself. He is his own witness as he
has been throughout his life. He is the Messiah,
the Redeemer, he who is sent to die, and he who is

willing to submit. This testimony is repeated two times by Christ, as is the question that brought it about. The arresting officers "went backward and fell to the ground," upon hearing his first testimony, "I am he." Their reaction adds credence to Christ's statement. Christ steps toward the cringing officers and repeats his question.

> Then asked he them again, *"Whom seek ye?* And they said, Jesus of Nazareth.
> Jesus answered, I have told you that *I am he*: if therefore ye seek me, let these go their way (John 18:7–8).

The significance of Christ's testimony is amplified by remembering several other times that Jesus used similar words. In chapter eight of John's Gospel, Christ ends his debate with the Jewish leaders with an identical proclamation. The Jews accuse Christ of claiming to be greater than Abraham.

> Your father Abraham rejoiced to see my day: and he saw it and was glad (John 8:56).

The Jews respond on a temporal level by telling Jesus, "Thou art not yet fifty years old, and hast thou seen Abraham?" Jesus then bears testimony of himself.

> Jesus said unto them, Verily, verily, I say unto you, Before Abraham was, I am (John 8:58).

John ends chapter eight with this simple pronouncement. Jesus has said all that needs to be said. In Exodus 3:14, Jehovah answered Moses inquiry from the burning bush with similiar words. At that occasion he said: "I am that I am." Remembering this past scriptural exclamation will greatly enhance the Savior's words to the Jewish leaders.

Other Gospel writers pick up on this usage of the testimony "I am." In Mark chapters fourteen and fifteen, the importance is stressed again. When asked by the Jewish leaders during his trial," Art thou the Christ, the Son of the Blessed?" Jesus answers plainly and powerfully, "I am" (Mark 14:62). Later when Pilate asks a similar question Jesus responds, "I am even as thou sayest" (Mark 15:2, J.S.T.). In light of all this the significance of the statements in the Garden of Gethsemane are enhanced.

As we have seen throughout John's Gospel, the Jews who oppose Christ are blind. They do not recognize that Christ is He who is to come, the great "I am." They do not seek him in the truest sense. They see him, but they do not see him as the Son of God.

Christ is then arrested and taken bound before Annas, Caiaphas' father–in–law. He is followed by Peter and John. John relates the three denials of Peter and a brief summation of Christ's trial before Annas. He is then led before Pilate.

There is a tone of irony in John's statement preceding the trial before Pilate.

> Then led they Jesus from
> Caiaphas unto the hall of judgment:
> and it was early; and they themselves
> went not into the judgment hall, lest
> they should be defiled; but that they
> might eat the passover (John 18:28).

What could defile them more than the crucifixion of he who came to save them? This scripture is reminiscent of one given earlier that the Jews went up to the passover "to purify themselves."

The trial before Pilate occupies the last verses of chapter eighteen and the first half of chapter nineteen. Pilate asks Jesus, "Art thou the King of the Jews?" As a Roman he is most concerned about challenge to Roman authority. John, ever conscious of the need to show the spiritual, deeper value of Christ's life, relates the Savior's answer to his question in some detail.

> Jesus answered, My kingdom is
> not of the world: if my kingdom were of
> this world, then would my servants
> fight, that I should not be delivered to
> the Jews; but now is my kingdom not
> from hence (John 18:36).

The whole of John's Gospel has been directed to proving that Christ's kingdom is not a worldly one. Pilate, as so many others we have met in

John's testimony, sees only earthly kingdoms and temporal issues. "Art thou a king then?" he asks. To which Christ answers:

> Thou sayest that I am a king. To this end was I born, and for this cause came I into the world, that I should bear witness unto the truth. Every one that is of the truth heareth my voice (John 18:37).

This is Christ's mission summed up by his own declaration. He came to bear witness of the truth. These are strong echoes of John's preface. Pilate then asks a critical question. "What is truth?" Once again we have a brief statement full of undertones and meanings. The dialogue ends here. John frequently ends his dialogues and conversations with powerful last words that invite examination and search. If we search for our own answer to his all important question, we will further understand John's power as one who testified of Christ's divinity. Earlier Christ testified of himself with these words, "I am the way, *the truth*, and the life."

"What is truth?" Pilate asks. John would answer that Jesus is the truth. He is "full of grace and truth." This John bore witness of in the first verses of chapter one. Christ told Pilate that he came to bear "witness unto the truth." He could have said, " I came to bear witness of myself for I am the truth." Many of the statements Christ made, throughout John's Gospel, bear witness to his own divinity.

If we ponder deep enough on this principle and theme, we will remember Christ's statements reported in chapter eight by John. Jesus said to his disciples at that moment:

> ...If ye continue in my word,
> then are ye my disciples indeed;
> And he shall know the truth,
> and the truth shall make you free
> (John 8:31–32).

This verse now takes on more profound meaning when seen in conjunction with others that Christ made regarding truth. Surely the truths of the Gospel make us free. But Christ is the truth. To continue in him by faith will free us from sin through his Atonement. Jesus told Pilate he came to bear witness unto the truth. What greater truth should he declare than the freedom from sin and death that comes through belief on his name. Christ could also say, "Ye shall know me and I will make you free."

After his initial questions, Pilate returns to the Jews and reports, "I find in him no fault at all." Again John gives us a sentence full of meaning. This is Pilate's testimony. We have heard many other's, from the Samaritan woman to Caiaphas himself. Christ was sinless. Literally "in him" was "no fault at all." John is careful to report that Pilate makes this statement more than once. This too was testified of in the preface where John told us Christ was "full of grace and truth." One who is full of grace and truth has no fault. There is no room in him for fault for he is "full." Throughout

John's narrative the Jews have tried to find a fault
in Christ in order to condemn him. They have
insulted him, mocked him and laid traps for him.
Now, just prior to his death, His judge proclaims,
"I find in him no fault at all." Pilate never said
truer words.

Pilate then attempts to appease the Jews and
save Jesus. He offers them a choice of Barabbas or
Jesus. In legal terms he is saying to them, "I will
condemn him as you wish, but then I will pardon
him." This does not work and Barabbas is released.
This too has symbolic meaning for the death and
condemnation of Christ releases the prisoners of
Satan and the grave as Barabbas is released from a
Roman prison.

JOHN CHAPTER NINETEEN
Behold the Man

Chapter nineteen begins with Pilate's
renewed attempts to save Christ. Pilate scourges
Jesus, a lesser sentence, in the hopes of sparing
him. Throughout all of Pilate's attempts there is
great irony. Here is the Judge of the world being
judged by the very people he came to save and being
defended by a representative of the earthly kingdom
(Rome), which kingdom the Jews wanted their
Messiah to lead them against.

After the scourging and mocking of the
soldiers, Pilate brings Jesus out again and says,
"Behold I bring him forth to you, that *ye may know*
that I find *no fault in him.* " Once again we have a
testimony given "that ye may know." John then
interrupts Pilate's words by saying, "Then came

Jesus forth...and Pilate saith unto them, *Behold the man!*" These are very powerful words coming from the lips of Pilate. They restate John's "seeing" theme all over. They echo his, "come and see" statements given earlier and John the Baptist's testimony heard in chapter one, "Behold the Lamb of God." John wants us to do exactly what Pilate demands. We should "Behold the Man." We should see that in him is no "fault at all," We are to see at this moment, the humility, love, and submission of the Son of God, not to the will of man or an earthly king, but to the will of a Father in Heaven. We are to see the Son in the midst of his Atonement. To make sure we do not miss this point John tells us of Christ's assurance to Pilate that "Thou couldst have no power at all against me, except it were given thee from above." Christ had totally submitted himself to his Father's will. Pilate is a minor character in this grand drama of the Atonement.

Pilate's desire to create sympathy for Jesus through the scourging fails. The Jews do not "behold the man," but cry for his death. They accuse him of blasphemy saying, "He made himself the Son of God," This disturbs Pilate who returns to ask Jesus, "Whence art thou?" John has answered this question also, throughout his Gospel. Christ has repeatedly told his listeners that he is from above and that he knew from "whence (he) came." The answer was first given in the preface where John introduced Christ as coming from God. We have seen it repeated often. Jesus, however, does not answer Pilate's question.

It should be clear by now to any reader how many themes are being alluded to in these final chapters. John creates a unified whole to all he has said earlier.

The Jews finally threaten Pilate by suggesting anyone who lets Christ go is not Caesar's friend. This causes Pilate to bring Christ out one more time. John tells us, "It was the preparation of the passover and about the sixth hour." This is an important detail. The "Lamb of God" is about to be offered by the high priest and the Jews. Pilate declares at this hour, "*Behold your king*." The invitation to see Christ one last time is given. The Jews do not comprehend their Messiah and he is led away to be crucified. This shows the ultimate truth of what John told us in the first verses of his testimony, "The world knew him not."

Today we need to "behold our king." We need to behold him giving us a living example of all he taught about love and obedience to the Father's will. This last invitation spoken by Pilate is a strong part of John's own testimony. The invitation is for all men to behold the king fighting to save his kingdom by his own death, saving his sheep by destroying their true enemy, Satan and the world. He is doing what he promised. "Be of good cheer, I have overcome the world." We will be part of his kingdom if we follow Jesus' example of love and sacrifice. We "behold our king" laying down his life as he promised he would.

The Jews cried out, "We have no king but Caesar." Thus they chose the world over the Savior, (an important theme of John), and "led him away" to Golgotha. John then gives us one final

testimony coming from the lips of Pilate. The Jews
complain about the writing over the cross. Pilate
has written, "Jesus of Nazareth, The King of the
Jews." To the complaining Jews who want the
writing to state he claimed to be the king, Pilate
answers, "What I have written I have written." He
was the "King."

John relates one special event from the cross,
that of Christ's concern for his mother. Speaking to
Mary and John, Jesus says:

> ...Woman, behold thy son!
> Then saith he to the disciple,
> Behold thy mother! And from that
> hour that disciple took her unto his
> own home (John 19:26–27).

Even at this moment of agony Christ
evidences his selfless love by his concern for the
care of his mother. Having related this John states:

> After this, Jesus knowing that
> all things were now accomplished, that
> the scripture might be fulfilled, saith, I
> thirst (John 19:28).

He is given vinegar which he receives. He
then says, "*It is finished*," and dies. He has obeyed
the Father's commandment and completed the
purpose for which he was born. The Resurrection
and his work in the spirit world await him. He will
"finish" these commandments also. The soldiers
come to break the condemned men's legs. John
records the piercing of Christ's side when they see

he is already dead. He details that piercing by
explaining, "...and forthwith came there out blood
and water." Then addressing himself personally to
his readers John bears his testimony to the actual
death of Christ. It is necessary for the reader to
know Christ truly died as a prelude to the
Resurrection that will soon be described.

> And he that saw it bare record,
> and his record is true: and he knoweth
> that he saith true, that ye might believe
> (John 19:35).

Nicodemus and Joseph of Arimathaea then
take Christ's body down and bury it in the garden.
They request his body "secretly for fear of the Jews."
Even now they cannot "walk in the light," giving
only token discipleship.

JOHN CHAPTER TWENTY
He Saw and Believed

Chapter twenty focuses entirely on the
Resurrection. We are given a number of testimonies concerning it. John's own comes first.
Mary Magdalene goes early to the tomb where she
sees the two angels sitting on the stone. She runs to
get Peter and John. They "ran both together; and
the other disciple did out run Peter and came first
to the sepulchre." John stoops down and looks into
the empty tomb and sees the grave clothes. These
he describes in considerable detail. When Peter
arrives they both enter the tomb. In a simple, yet
moving statement John bears his own testimony

indicating that at last he has finally seen the truth of Christ's mission. John states simply these words, "*He saw* and believed." This is followed by an explanation.

> For as yet they knew not the scripture, that he must rise again from the dead (John 20:9).

We would assume from this that John is the first to bear testimony of the Resurrected Christ—the first to see and believe. John can be contrasted with Thomas, who demands physical seeing before believing as so many others did and do today.

The Apostles leave Mary weeping. She sees the two angels who ask her the cause of her sorrow. "Because they have taken away my Lord and I know not where they have laid him." At this moment Mary then turns, and the scriptures tell us, she "...saw Jesus standing, and knew not that it was Jesus." Mary is looking at Jesus, but does not recognize him. Jesus then issues the questions he asked John and Andrew the first time he met them and the same question he offered the arresting officers in Gethsemane. "Woman, why weepest thou? Whom seekest thou?" Who are you seeking? Mary is not yet aware, but the one she seeks is standing in front of her. This is true of all men. The one we seek is in plain sight, but we must see him with eyes of faith and love. Mary has that love and recognizes the Master when he gently calls her name. There follows a moment of deep comfort and joy. Joseph Smith changes the words, "Touch me not," to "Hold me not," meaning don't detain me for "I ascend unto my Father and your Father; and to my God and your God."   The unity of Christ with the Father and the Father with his children is stressed. Because of Christ's ascent to "his Father" all of mankind is presented with that same possibility.

Let us here digress slightly from the text of John and turn to Luke twenty–four where we read of a similar experience. The Luke experience of the two disciples on the road to Emmaus marks clearly the "seeing" theme. As the two disciples discuss in sorrow the events of the last few days, Jesus draws near to them. Luke then says, "But their *eyes were holden* that they should *not know him*." Christ questions the two disciples and is told of the crucifixion, the death, and the women's testimony "that he was alive." The two disciples then make reference to the visit of Peter and John to the tomb.

> And certain of them which were with us went to the sepulchre and found it even so as the women had said: but him they saw not (Luke 24:24).

The unbelief of the disciples is rebuked by Christ. "O fools, and slow of heart to believe all that the prophets have spoken: Ought not Christ to have suffered these things, and to enter into his glory?" Their literal inability to see and "know" Christ is but an outward sign of their lack of belief and understanding of his true mission.   Christ then, beginning at "Moses and all the prophets," expounds "unto them in all the scriptures the things concerning himself." Jesus has attempted to open the eyes of the disciples to a fuller understanding of his mission by teaching them out of the scriptures. They arrive at Emmaus and request the Savior to "abide with (them)." He sits at their table, breaks bread and gives it to them.

> And their *eyes were opened* , and *they knew him*; and he vanished out of their sight.
> And they said one to another, Did not our heart burn within us, while he talked with us by the way, and while he opened to us the scriptures? (Luke 24:31–32).

The opening of the scriptures and the burning in the hearts have helped them to see and know Christ, because they finally understand the prophetic fulfillment of his life. When their hearts have received the knowledge and understanding of Christ's true mission the outward blindness is removed. They see Him.

This is a perfect example of what John's testimony will accomplish. The reading of the scriptures, particularly John, is for us now, a way to have our eyes opened. It is an opportunity to look at the Savior's life, Atonement, and gospel, and feel our hearts burn within us as we understand the perfect example Christ set and the power of his Atonement. If we read John and comprehend his description of Christ, we will share in the disciple's

experience, and our hearts will burn within us.
Then we too will see him and know him.

Returning to chapter twenty of John we read
of one more man who needs to see Christ in order to
believe. That man is Thomas. On the day of
Christ's Resurrection the disciples are "assembled
for fear of the Jews." Jesus comes to them, stands
in their midst and "saith unto them, Peace be unto
you." He then "shewed them his hands and his
side. Then were the disciples glad, when they saw
the Lord." The realization of his true mission has
dawned on them. They understand. They have
seen the Lord.

Thomas is not present. When told of the
appearance of Christ he refuses to believe. His faith
is not like John's who believed after he saw the
empty tomb. "Except I shall see in his hands the
prints of the nails...I will not believe," Thomas
declares. Eight days later Christ returns to the
other disciples and Thomas. Christ invites Thomas
to, "Reach hither thy finger, and behold my
hands...and be not faithless, but believing."
Thomas answers, "My Lord and my God." Thomas
has seen and now believes in the Resurrected
Christ. Only now does he understand this vital part
of the Savior's mission, a part before uncom-
prehended. We should not be overly harsh on
Thomas. The other Apostles did not believe the
testimony of the women which they bore the
morning of the Resurrection.

After Thomas' testimony Christ mildly
rebukes him for his unbelief. In his rebuke we read
of another type of seeing.

> Jesus saith unto him, Thomas, because thou hast seen me, thou hast believed: blessed are they that have not seen, and yet have believed (John 20:29).

The promise is given that seeing the Savior in truth need not be accomplished with the eyes, but with the heart and spirit. There will be those in the future who will be blessed because they see Christ without physical evidence. This is the seeing of faith that Christ alluded to while talking to Nicodemus. Those who are born again or born of the Spirit will see Christ and his kingdom without outward signs or manifestation. This is a truth John has testified of throughout his Gospel.

John follows up his testimony of Christ's Resurrection with a restatement of his purpose. "These are written that ye might believe that Jesus is the Christ, the Son of God." If the reader has comprehended the depth of seeing John described, he or she will believe, and with "believing...have life through his name."

This appears to be a logical end to John's Gospel. Some have thought chapter twenty–one was not written by John or that if written by him, was added as an afterthought. However, if we remember the purpose of John's writing and the emphasis given to seeing and love, the twenty–first chapter fits perfectly and provides a final emphasis to all John desires.

JOHN CHAPTER TWENTY ONE
Feed My Sheep

Chapter twenty–one centers on an appearance of Christ by the Sea of Galilee and the subsequent conversation. This pattern of event and commentary has been readily seen before in many of John's previous chapters. Peter and certain other apostles "go a fishing." This is done at Peter's suggestion. They fish all night and catch nothing. When the morning comes Christ is standing on the shore, "but the disciples knew not that it was Jesus." This could be a repeat of the road–to–Emmaus blindness and that of Mary in the garden or it could simply be a matter of distance to the shore. We cannot be sure with the scriptural information. Jesus tells them to "cast the net on the right side of the ship, and ye shall find." The resultant catch is enormous.

Christ has repeated an earlier miracle recorded in Luke chapter five. After the huge catch of fish in that earlier story Jesus issued the call, "Come follow me and I will make you fishers of men." This present episode is a gentle hint. Are the Apostles returning to their nets to fish for fish or will they truly follow the Savior and fish for men? We saw earlier in the Last Supper the strong emphasis on love for Christ and our fellowmen. The manifestation of love for both Christ and others is shown in the preaching of the gospel. Christ's repetition of an earlier miracle is a redirection to that purpose.

John recognizes the Savior first. Perhaps he remembers the former miracle. He tells Peter, "It is the Lord." Peter jumps into the sea in his eagerness to be with Jesus. There follows a simple meal and then the all important conversation between Jesus and Peter.

> So when they had dined, Jesus saith to Simon Peter, Simon, son of Jonas, lovest thou me more than these? He saith unto him, Yea, Lord; thou knowest that I love thee. He saith unto him, Feed my lambs.
> He saith to him again the second time, Simon, son of Jonas, Lovest thou me? He saith unto him, Yea, Lord; thou knowest that I love thee. He saith unto him, Feed my sheep.
> He saith unto him the third time, Simon, son of Jonas, lovest thou me? Peter was grieved because he said unto him the third time, Lovest thou me? and he said unto him, Lord, thou knowest all things; thou knowest that I love thee. Jesus saith unto him, Feed my sheep (John 21:15–17).

Three times the question is asked. Three times comes the command to "Feed my sheep." The message is strong and obvious. At the Last Supper, Christ told the Apostles to keep his commandments if they loved him. The most important commandment he could give since he was to ascend to the Father, was the feeding of his sheep. In this way the Apostles would manifest love for Christ, the Father, and the sheep. This is a sign of a truly converted disciple. To truly see Christ is to see the importance of this commandment, for in following it we not only do the work of Christ, we become like him.

Jesus asked Peter the first time if he loved him "more than these?" What was he referring to? Perhaps one of two things. The "these" could refer to the fish that Peter personally pulled to the shore. If so the question, "Lovest thou me more than these?" implies a love of Christ beyond the earthly pursuits of life. Peter was to accomplish a more important mission than the accumulating of worldly accomplishments. If our heart is on Christ, the things of the world will never hold us back from feeding the sheep.

Another interpretation works just as well and perhaps better correlates with the rest of John's Gospel and the truths taught in the First Epistle. The "these" may refer to the other brethren present. If this is the case Jesus is asking Peter if he loves him more than his fellowman. The commandment to feed the sheep may be a suggestion that Peter love the sheep as much as he loves the Savior. That love will be manifested in his care for the sheep. This second thought is strongly taught in the First Epistle. Both meanings are powerful and the ambiguity is not entirely undesired.

Chapter twenty–one ends with the suggestion that John will not see death, but tarry until Christ returns. This seems a fitting end to John's Gospel and is certainly a capstone to chapter twenty–one. Why does John wish to remain? We can find the answer to this question in the Doctrine and Covenants, section seven, which contains more information about the conversations of John twenty–one. John asks the Savior:

> Lord, give unto me power over death, that I may live and bring souls unto thee (D&C 7:2).

John wishes to remain in order to fulfill the Savior's commandment to feed the sheep. John's love is great for both the Savior and the sheep. He is willing to forego a quick entrance into Christ's kingdom because of his great love. For centuries he will bring souls to Christ. Jesus then says:

> My beloved has desire that he might do more, or a greater work yet among men than what he has before done (D&C 7:5).

John's desire to do a "greater work" indicates that, perhaps, he saw the Savior more clearly than anyone. His love was truly Christlike and this may explain why he was called by Jesus the "beloved" disciple. No one was so close to his heart and purposes. John was one with Christ in a very special way. The final testimony of John is the assurance that true conversion, true discipleship comes from being like Christ, doing all that we can to follow him.

The last words of John's testimony contain the truth that all the world could not "contain the books that should be written" about all that Christ was and did. How ironic that the Christian world

quotes John's last words in Revelation about adding
to the Bible instead of these last words. John used
the word "should" be written. Apparently John
himself lamented the fact that too little was said
about Jesus, his teachings, his life, his gospel, and
his Atonement. This last verse of John's should be
the verse the Christian world quotes. Then they
would have rejoiced when another Testament of
Christ came forth. This lack of understanding
leading to the rejection of further revelation is
another indication that many Christians still have
not seen the Christ.

  Chapters twenty and twenty–one were
written very powerfully. They were intended to
stamp on our minds the two main aspects of a
testimony of Christ—that of truly seeing his
mission and life, and that of love and service. The
first leads naturally to the second. Chapter twenty
forcefully declares that Jesus was the divine Son of
God who came to the earth to atone and bring the
gift of the Resurrection and eternal life to all men.
Chapter twenty–one teaches the truth that a true
disciple of Christ will, through his love of Christ
and his fellowman, feed the sheep the bread of the
gospel and the living water of truth. The true
disciple will teach the world of Christ's Atonement,
that all can have faith, be converted, and win
exaltation.

  I hope a few concluding thoughts will not be
inappropiate. John's Gospel can serve as a
touchstone for all generations if men will apply the
principles contained within the major themes to
themselves. Many people and organizations today

claim to "see" Christ, but far too often they exhibit the characteristics of those who opposed him from the beginning. They see their traditions, not the Son. They refuse to accept the added truths he has given. They condemn, in his name, the vast majority of God's children past and present to an endless hell for not believing in his name in the exact way they believe in it. In like manner they condemm those who lived in a time and place where the name of Christ was not preached. Through their wars, fought in his name, they have destroyed millions of his brothers and sisters, and enslaved in ignorance and chains vast regions of the globe. Their doctrines create confusion and contention, condemn the innocent child, deny the literal reality of his Resurrection, confuse and twist his oneness with the Father, and silence him forever with their cry, "A Bible, a Bible. We have got a Bible, and there cannot be any more Bible." Through it all the simple truths of love, meekness, and sacrifice have often been forgotten. Truly the psalmist described them in the following words:

> But unto the wicked God saith, What hast thou to do to declare my statutes, or that thou shouldest take my covenant in thy mouth?
>
> Seeing thou hatest instruction, and castest my words behind thee.
>
> Thou givest thy mouth to evil, and thy tongue frameth deceit.
>
> Thou sittest and speakest against thy brother; thou slanderest thine own mother's son.

These things hast thou done,
and I kept silence; thou thoughtest that
I was altogether such an one as
thyself: but I will reprove thee, and set
covenants in order before thine eyes
(Psalms 50:16–17, 19–21 JST).

The scripture said, "Thou thoughtest that I
was altogether such an one as thyself." What an
ironic statement. In his apostasy man remakes
God in his own image, instead of allowing God to
remake him in the image of his Son. In the First
Epistle John promises we shall be like Christ if we
love and keep the commandments. The world has
reversed the order and made Christ like
themselves. In Revelation John will take this
theme and teach it to the fullest. Is this not what
the Jews did to their concept of the Messiah? But
John has provided us with his own testimony and
wherever a man or woman or child reads it with
meekness and sincerity they will see the Savior and
know his love and in that vision they will see their
fellowman and love "the sheep," not condemn
them. They will mold themselves in the patterns
established by the Master instead of molding him to
fit their own preconceived prejudices. Though we
may have lost some of the "plain and precious"
truths (1 Nephi 14:23) once found in John's
writings, the power and testimony is still there for
those "who have eyes to see."

CHAPTER FOUR

Doctrine & Covenants Section 93

Whenever one has searched for insights in the scriptures and reached certain conclusions, one should test, inasmuch as possible, those conclusions with other prophetic truths. One should test them with other scriptures, the statements of living prophets and the whisperings of the Holy Ghost.

In the foregoing pages we have studied the testimony of John the Beloved concerning Christ. The study was not extensive, but focused on a few ideas that seem to be central to John's purposes and the Savior's life. We examined his emphasis on *coming,* and *seeing* Christ and His full mission. We saw the repeated emphasis on Christ as the light of the world—a light one needed to see, and a light by which we see all things. We discussed John's emphasis of the Father/Son relationship, their oneness and the invitation that is extended to all humanity to share in that oneness. We saw the repeated use of the verb "to know" and the manner one can know the Father and the Son. We learned

that part of Christ's mission was to reveal to us the
nature and character of the Father. We stressed
the truth that seeing and knowing Christ is the
same as seeing and knowing the Father. Lastly, we
saw the emphasis John placed on love. He taught
us that Christ's love took basic forms: 1. A love of
obedience to God's commandments, especially the
commandment to atone; and, 2. A love for his
sheep, his friends, and for all of his brothers and
sisters. This love caused him to lay down his life.
Both loves brought to the world the saving truths of
his gospel. And we learned that Christ expects that
same kind of love from us if we are to be his
disciples.

Let us take these basic themes and truths
from John's testimony and examine them in light
of another scripture closely associated with John.
Section ninety–three of the Doctrine and Covenants
contains scriptures that parallel those given by
John in his preface.

A close reading of Doctrine and Covenants
ninety–three seems to indicate that the John
referred to means John the Baptist. If so, we can
conclude that John the Beloved used a now unkown
scriptural record of the Baptist in writing his own
preface. This is not hard to understand if we
remember John was a disciple of the Baptist before
he followed Christ.

Let us now look at the parallels section
ninety–three gives us to John's Gospel emphasis.

Therefore, in the beginning the
Word was, for he was the Word, even
the messenger of salvation—

The light and the Redeemer of the world; the Spirit of truth, who came into the world, because the world was made by him, and in him was the life of men and the light of men.

The worlds were made by him; men were made by him ; all things were made by him, and through him, and of him.

And I, John, bear record that I beheld his glory, as the glory of the Only Begotten of the Father, full of grace and truth, even the Spirit of truth, which came and dwelt in the flesh, and dwelt among us (D&C 93:8–11).

It is easy to see the close similarity of these verses to John chapter one. They are followed by a testimony that Christ did not receive "of the fulness at first," but received "grace for grace." We learn that Christ's continuing from grace to grace led to his receiving "a fulness."

For the purpose of our present study, the verses preceding and following the above truths are most interesting. The Savior himself, begins section ninety–three, giving his own introduction to the testimony John used to begin his Gospel. Christ teaches the following truths.

Verily, thus saith the Lord: It shall come to pass that every soul who forsaketh his sins and *cometh unto me*, and calleth on my name, and

> obeyeth my voice, and *keepeth my*
> *commandments, shall see my face and*
> *know that I am*;
> And that *I am the true light that*
> *lighteth every man* that cometh into the
> world;
> And that *I am in the Father*, and
> the Father in me, and *the Father and I*
> *are one—*
> I was in the world and received
> of my Father, and *the works of him*
> *were plainly manifest* (D&C 93:1–3, 5).

Notice in these verses how many of John's themes
are touched on. (1.) If we come unto Christ and
obey him we shall see his face and know him. This,
I believe, is a literal promise; (2.) He is the true light
that lights all men's paths; and, (3.) He and his
Father are one, and through the works of Christ,
the Father, and the Father's works are "plainly
manifest."

These verses are followed by those quoted
earlier paralleling John's preface. The Savior then
comments further.

> I give unto you these sayings
> that you may understand and know
> how to worship, and know what you
> worship, that you may come unto the
> Father in my name, and in due time
> receive of his fulness.
> For if you keep my command-
> ments *you shall receive of his fulness*,
> and be glorified in me as I am in the

Father; therefore, I say unto you, *you shall receive grace for grace* (D&C 93:19–20).

These are powerful teachings and promises. Christ explains that he has given us the preceding verses to teach us: (1.) How to worship, and, (2.) What we worship. This is the same purpose for John's Gospel. His detailed explanation of Christ's purity and his desire for us to see the Savior is given in order for us to know what or who we worship. John's Gospel also tells us how to worship. We worship by becoming like Christ, by growing grace for grace, as he did. The key to this transformation is love, both the love that brings obedience to all of God's commandments and the love for our fellowmen that causes us to serve them and share with them the truths of the Gospel.

In summation then, how do we truly worship Christ? We worship him by becoming like him. How do we do that? The answer is found both in Doctrine and Covenants, section ninety–three and John's Gospel. "You become like Christ through obedience and love." Section ninety–three gives added testimony to the consistency of John's message and the true way to become exalted. Using Doctrine and Covenants section ninety–three we can simplify John's purposes into two main objectives, which are the same as the Lord's. We need to know who we worship and how to worship him. John has provided the answers if we have eyes to see. He will continue to supply the answers in his First Epistle where we will see the same themes emerging. Then in the Revelation he will present us with a choice. We can know the Savior and how to worship him or we can know the adversary and how to worship him. All of John's writings show a consistency and a concentration of those points most critical for mankind.

CHAPTER FIVE

The Epistles of John

Love or Contention—The Spirit of a Disciple or the Spirit of an Anti–Christ.

To understand the Epistles it is well to remember some of the major focuses of John's Gospel. John used the verb "to see" repeatedly. He wanted those who read his testimony to see the Savior's true mission. John emphasized the oneness of Christ with the Father. He spoke of the invitation Christ's Atonement presented for all men to become one with each other and the Savior, and therefore one with the Father also. John also dealt in detail with the type of pure love true disciples possess. Christ's love was made manifest for both his Father and mankind through his Atonement. With these major themes in mind it is not difficult to understand the Epistles. Within a few verses of the First Epistle we see all these themes tied together, as we saw them in section ninety–three of the Doctrine and Covenants.

1 JOHN

Early in the First Epistle's introduction John testifies, "We have seen with our eyes...we have looked...and our hands have handled of the word of life." John is always testifying. One can believe his witness because he has "seen" the Christ. He knows of the reality of his Resurrection. John continues his introduction.

> That which we have seen and heard declare we unto you, that ye also may have fellowship with us: and truly our fellowship is with the Father, and with his Son Jesus Christ.
> And these things write we unto you, that your joy may be full (1 John 1:3–4).

The purpose of his Epistle is to reissue the invitation of Christ given so beautifully in the Intercessory Prayer, that of unity with the Father and Son. This was also seen in section ninety–three. In the present epistle, fellowship with the Apostles will lead to fellowship with both the Father and the Son. This is contingent on following the Apostle's counsel and receiving a testimony. This fellowship will produce the "joy" mentioned in verse four. There can be no true joy in isolation from the Father and Son. A major purpose, therefore, of John's First Epistle is to teach us how to maintain a "fellowship" with the Father and Son.

John's emphasis on light is seen in the next verse. "God is light and in him is no darkness at all." The suggestion of John is apparent. If we become one with Christ and the Father, there will be no darkness in us either. In fact, one of the ways to know a true disciple will be the intensity of "light" which is radiated. This brings us to a main concern found in John's First Epistle. How do we tell a true disciple of Christ? The apostasy was well underway by the time this epistle was written. John felt considerable anxiety about the membership of the Church. This same anxiety resurfaced in the first chapters of the Revelation. The First Epistle's purpose was to both warn and exhort the members to maintain the unity and love with each other and the Father. This unity was a sign of the true Church.

John began this warning and exhortation by continuing his emphasis on light. God has no darkness in him. Therefore "if we say we have fellowship with him and walk in darkness, we lie." We cannot be one with God and embrace darkness. By contrast John continues, "But if we walk in the light as he is in the light, we have fellowship one with another." Notice the emphasis on unity with each other. Walking in the light will produce a oneness with our fellowmen, especially with other believers. This becomes a sign of the true believers. John is merely echoing a teaching of the Savior. "If ye are not one ye are not mine."

John concluded chapter one with a reference to the "darkness" or sin an individual may claim to be free of and therefore deceives others and himself.

> If we say that we have no sin, we
> deceive ourselves, and the truth is not
> in us.
>
> If we confess our sins, he is
> faithful and just to forgive us our sins,
> and to cleanse us from all
> unrighteousness (1 John 1:8–9).

Thus all have need of Christ to form true fellowship. Christ invites all to receive of his mercy. Through humility, repentance, confession and faith, the darkness of any individual will be purged by "light." This theme continues in chapter two. It is here made clear that the Atonement is meant to include "the sins of the whole world," for Christ came to save the whole world. In his Gospel, John emphasized the infinite reach of the Atonement. It is restated in the First Epistle lest the believers take on the prejudiced intolerant attitude of the Pharisees who believed that they were the chosen, loved and elected favorites of God.

John returns to the signs of a true believer. In the Intercessory Prayer, Christ stated that "life eternal" was "to know" Christ and God. How will we know that we know them and have received the blessings of Christ's Atonement? John answers:

> And hereby we do know that we
> know him, if we keep his
> commandments.
>
> He that saith, I know him, and
> keepeth not his commandments, is a
> liar, and the truth is not in him (1
> John 2:3–4).

This is a repeat of the teachings of Christ at the Last Supper and Intercessory Prayer. The keeping of the commandments is an indication of a true disciple, but there is one commandment that is critical. It is, "The new commandment," Christ gave at the Last Supper to "love one another." If we keep this commandment "the love of God" is "perfected" in us and we will "walk even as he walked." In other words we "know" the Father and the Son through our desire and ability to do and feel the things they do and feel, literally to "walk" their pathways. John then emphasizes the "new commandment" indicating that in reality it is not new but the very foundation of a Christian's belief.

> Brethren, I write a new commandment unto you, but it is the same commandment which ye had from the beginning. The old commandment is the word which ye have heard from the beginning (JST 1 John 2:7).

John is now ready to tie his ideas together by returning to his reference to "light." We are now able to understand more deeply what this light represents and what it brings.

> He that saith he is in the light, and hateth his brother, is in darkness even until now.
> He that loveth his brother abideth in the light, and there is none occasion of stumbling in him.

> But he that hateth his brother is
> in darkness, and walketh in darkness,
> and knoweth not whither he goeth,
> because that darkness hath blinded his
> eyes (1 John 2:9–11).

To walk in the light is to have a Christlike love.
Light and charity become synonymous. As light
and darkness cannot exist together, so love and hate
cannot exist in the same heart at the same time.
John is giving us an extremely important, but
simple, principle for our modern times. In a world
of confusion concerning the true identity of Christ's
church and disciples, one should look for the "light"
of love and unity. The persecutions, wars, hatreds,
intolerances and condemnations of the various
Christian factions indicate they are not Christ's
because they are not "one." They do not see by the
light of his love. All of the above bear strong
testimony to the apostasy which took men away
from the true light of Christ. Hatred, darkness and
the lack of oneness indicate a turning away from
Christ to the world for these are the fruits of the
world. These same principles were taught by
Christ to Nicodemus when he spoke of those who do
deeds of darkness or evil. Their deeds are
indications that they have not come to light, but
"loved darkness."
    John, therefore, turns his attention to the
"world," apostasy, and the spirit of the
"anti–Christs." These three go hand in hand, and
he warns the members to avoid them, for they are
the spirit of darkness.

> Love not the world, neither the
> things that are in the world. If any
> man love the world, the love of the
> Father is not in him.
> For all that is in the world, the
> lust of the flesh, and the lust of the
> eyes, and the pride of life, is not of the
> Father, but is of the world (1 John
> 2:15–16).

To be one with the world breaks the oneness with the Father. The scriptures teach that no unclean thing dwells in the presence of the Father. They also teach that God cannot look upon sin in any degree of allowance. To embrace the world is to turn one's back on the Father. John knows that this is taking place in the Church. He, therefore, continues his exhortation by indicating the presence of the "anti–Christ."

> Little children, it is the last time:
> and as ye have heard that antichrist
> shall come, even now are there many
> antichrists; whereby we know that it is
> the last time.
> They went out from us, but they
> were not of us; for if they had been of
> us, they would no doubt have continued
> with us: but they went out, that they
> might be made manifest that they were
> not all of us (1 John 2:18–19).

John teachs that there are two truths we need to understand about the "anti–Christ": (1.) the spirit

of anti–Christ is a spirit of apostasy brought on by a
love of the world; and, (2.) the spirit of anti–Christ
is a spirit of dissension, hatred, contention and
disharmony, for all of these break the unity of a true
disciple and are therefore antichrist. Both of these
also break the oneness and love with the Father and
the Son and indicate a spirit of darkness. When one
is in darkness he cannot see the Son. John has
already taught that if we are not one with the
Father and Son, we will not be one with our
fellowmen. The result will be a continuation of the
long, sad song of man's inhumanity. Apostasy, as
a spirit of antichrist, breaks the oneness with God
by forming a oneness with the world. Since "the
world" has always hated the truth and the light, it
will always be antichrist. Jesus told the apostles at
the Last Supper, "I have chosen you out of the
world, therefore the world hateth you" (John 15:19).
We cannot love the world and love Christ too.

Love and oneness are the essence of Christ's
teachings, his light. Therefore, a spirit of
contention, hatred, intolerance, etc., is a spirit
contrary to the Savior. It is anti–Christ because it
represents everything Jesus opposes. It will be
important to remember these truths while reading
the Revelation. These two examples of anti–Christ,
that of apostasy with the world and that of
disharmony and hatred, are closely related to each
other. Notice how the prophet Joseph Smith tied the
two together while writing from Liberty jail.

It is an imperative duty that we
owe to God, to angels, with whom we
shall be brought to stand, and also to

ourselves, to our wives and children, who have been made to bow down with grief, sorrow, and care, under the most damning hand of *murder, tyranny,* and *oppression, supported and urged on and upheld by the influence of that spirit which hath so strongly riveted the creeds of the fathers, who have inherited lies, upon the hearts of the children, and filled the world with confusion,* and has been growing stronger and stronger, and *is now the very mainspring of all corruption,* and the whole earth groans under the weight of its iniquity.

It is an iron yoke, it is a strong band; they are the very handcuffs, and chains, and shackles, and fetters of hell (D&C 123:7–8).

John senses this movement away from Christ's love toward the world and its contentions. The First Epistle has great relevance for us today. This relevancy reaches its fruition in the Revelation where apostasy, the world, and hatred bring about the final downfall of "Babylon." In the Revelation the forces of light and darkness are starkly contrasted in perfect Apocalyptic style, but we will see that later.

John next indicates one last form of anti–Christ—that of overt denial. Apostasy and contention often lead to it.

> Who is a liar but he that denieth
> that Jesus is the Christ? He is
> antichrist, that denieth the Father and
> the Son.
> Whosoever denieth the Son, the
> same hath not the Father: [but] he that
> acknowledgeth the Son hath the Father
> also (1 John 2:22–23).

The overt denial of Christ is an easy anti–Christ to
see, but as we have learned, there are many ways to
"deny" the Father and the Son. Apostasy and lack
of love represent some of those ways. John exhorts
his followers to continue strong in the knowledge of
the truth of Christ in the face of anti–Christs.

> Let that therefore abide in you,
> which ye have heard from the
> beginning. If that which ye have heard
> from the beginning shall remain in
> you, ye also shall continue in the Son,
> and in the Father (1 John 2:24).

From the beginning, disciples have been taught the
truths of Christ's mission and the necessity to love
and obey. In love, unity, true vision of the Savior's
character and mission, and obedience, they will
receive "the promise of eternal life."
Since the promise of eternal life is extended
by Christ, John proceeds to elaborate on its
meaning and how to endure in order to receive the
final fulfillment. He first speaks of an anointing
they received.

> But the anointing which ye have
> received of him abideth in you and ye
> need not that any man teach you: but
> as the same anointing teacheth you of
> all things, and is truth, and is no lie,
> and even as it hath taught you, ye shall
> abide in him (1 John 2:27).

This is a reference to the gift of the Holy Ghost
which, if followed, will lead them to eternal life.
The Holy Ghost will help them endure. Giving heed
to the spirit will give one confidence until one can
stand in God's presence. The Holy Ghost will aid
one to hold fast to the truths received, to maintain
the unity of love, and to continue to see the true
character and mission of the Son.

This brings us to chapter three and a fuller
understanding of what eternal life involves. John
starts out with a reference to God's love. That love
is manifested in our being "called the sons of God."
What does the term "sons of God" have to do with
eternal life? John answers with a magnificent
promise.

> Beloved, now are we the sons of
> God, and it doth not yet appear what we
> shall be: but we know that, when he
> shall appear, we shall be like him; for
> we shall see him as he is (1 John 3:2).

Eternal life is life like God's and like Christ's. This
is the ultimate fulfillment of the invitation to be one
with the Father and Son as they are one. Christ
became one with God by proceeding from grace to

grace, as can all the "sons of God." If we believe this it will give us the courage and faith to overcome the spirit of anti–Christ. John explains:

> And every man that hath this
> hope in him purifieth himself, even as
> he is pure (1 John 3:3).

John now returns us to the basic truth introduced in the first of the Epistle. "Whosoever continueth in sin hath not seen him neither known him." Our outward actions will manifest our inward state. The sons of God will be like Christ. The Holy Ghost will help to purify them. They will not continue in sin. A "son of God" is one who "is born of God." A sign of his rebirth is his refusal to "continue in sin". This leads to a constant refinement of his character, until he is pure and becomes like the father of his spiritual rebirth—Christ. This is what it means to take the name of Christ. John testifies in all his writings that oneness with Christ equals oneness with the Father. Thus, becoming like Christ, or like the father of our rebirth, is the sign of a true disciple. John explains this in the following verse.

> In this the children of God are
> manifest, and the children of the devil:
> whosoever doeth not righteousness is
> not of God, neither he that loveth not
> his brother (1 John 3:10).

Earlier in the letter, John told his readers to hold to the truths that they "heard from the beginning."

He re–emphasizes that exhortation, supplying the specific truth they had "heard." He stresses that truth again, making it a major aspect of "purity" and "righteousness."

> For this is the message that ye
> heard from the beginning, that we
> should love one another (1 John 3:11).

Love is still the focus, the true sign of a converted individual. This love, as we saw taught at the Last Supper, will cause the "world [to] hate you." John uses an illustration—that of Cain and Abel. This first murder was done because Abel's works were righteous. Persecution of the righteous is, there-fore, another sign of an anti–Christ.

John now enters the major thrust of the Epistle. Principle after principle is laid down until a solid foundation of love and discipleship is explained. Notice the emphasis and relationship of the following quotations.

> ...He that loveth not his brother
> abideth in death (1 John 3:14).

To what extent must I love my brother? John answers that I must love him in the fullest sense of selfless sacrifice as Christ did.

> Hereby perceive we the love of
> God, because he laid down his life for
> us: and we ought to lay down our lives
> for the brethren (1 John 3:16).

John shows the practical day–by–day applications
of love in the following verse.

> But whoso hath this world's
> goods, and seeth his brother have need,
> and shutteth up his bowels of
> compassion from him, how dwelleth
> the love of God in him? (1 John 3:17).

John then pleads for true love, not lip service.

> My little children, let us not love
> in words, neither in tongue; but in deed
> and in truth (1 John 3:18).

The last of the chapter is devoted to the promise that
we will have "confidence toward God" if we
continue in the love and unity described above.
Whatever we ask the Father he will give because we
"do those things that are pleasing in his sight."
This verse is a quote of a statement made by Christ
and recorded by John in his Gospel. Jesus said, "I
do always those things that please him." He is now
applying it to all disciples who seek unity with the
Father and Son. The Father can give the true
disciple whatever he asks, because he will always
ask what is right or "pleasing." A good example of
this is found in the Book of Mormon when the Lord
tells Nephi II:

> And now, because thou hast
> done this with such unwearyingness,
> behold, I will bless thee forever; and I
> will make thee mighty in word and in

deed, in faith and in works; yea, even
that all things shall be done unto thee
according to thy word, *for thou shalt
not ask that which is contrary to my
will* (Helaman 10:5).

Nephi III has reached a state of oneness in will
with Christ. It is selfless love and obedience that
enables God to place this total confidence in his
"sons" and "daughters."

The teachings on love continue in chapter
four. John alludes once again to "false spirits" and
"false prophets." We are not to fear them or the
world because "greater is he that is in you than he
that is in the world."

Beloved, let us love one another:
for love is of God;, and every one that
loveth is *born of God*, and knoweth
God.

He that loveth not knoweth not
God; for *God is love*.

In this was manifested the love
of God toward us, because that God
sent his only begotten Son into the
world, that we might live through him.

Herein is love, not that we loved
God, but that he loved us, and sent his
Son to be the propitiation for our sins.

Beloved, *if God so loved us we
ought also to love one another* (1 John
4:7–11).

Herein we find a central kernel of truth—God is
love. The Father is the source of all love. He is so
filled with love that his name becomes synonymous
with love. Love is the key element in being "born of
God." God's love was manifest in the Atonement as
much as was the Savior's. So far John has
emphasized the love of the Savior and the love of
man for his fellowmen. Now he tells us of the
Father's love. The Father does not demand of his
Son or of us anything that he does not already
possess in its fullest sense. We have been told to
follow the Savior's example of love. Now we are told
to follow the Father's example of love. Love becomes
a unifying force in the oneness of the Father and
Son. We are admonished to let their example
become our own.

Following these verses, John gives several
promises that are fulfilled in those who love their
neighbor as the Father and Son love. In verse
twelve we are promised that God will dwell in us.
"His love is perfected in us" if we "love one
another." This promise is enlarged upon in verse
sixteen. "God is love; and he that dwelleth in love
dwelleth in God and God in him." Not only does
God dwell in us but we dwell in him in similar
relationship to that of the Father and Son. Verse
seventeen continues to build on the previous
promise. If God dwells in me and I in him, my love
will be perfected in my own exaltation and
perfection.

Herein is our love made perfect,
that we may have boldness in the day of

> judgment: because as he is, so are we
> in this world (1 John 4:17).

As Christ and the Father are, so we become. As
they are pure, we are pure. As Christ is one with
the Father, so we may become one through our love.
This knowledge brings the next promise.
"There is no fear in love; but perfect love casteth out
fear...he that feareth is not made perfect in love."
John is teaching that fear and love, just as hate and
love, cannot exist in the same heart at the same
time. Fear is basically a selfish emotion. Perfect
love is not centered on self, but on others. If my life
is centered in God and my fellowmen, fear will have
no root in my heart. Perfect love has faith in God
and Christ because of the oneness produced. For
these reasons, fear is absent, overcome by love.
As a final point of emphasis, John returns to
the practical issue of loving one's brother and links
it with seeing.

> If a man say, I love God, and
> hateth his brother, he is a liar: for he
> that loveth not his brother whom he
> hath seen, how can he love God whom
> he hath not seen (1 John 4:20).

There is more implied in the word "seen" than the
surface would indicate. I have not really seen God
if I hate my brother. Because "God is love" my
hatred of my brother is an indication of my lack of
understanding of the most basic truth about God.
But if I love my brother, that love enables me, by my
own experience, to comprehend my Father in

Heaven. All disciples who claim to be true followers
of Christ should be judged by John's standard of
love.

Chapter five contains the concluding truths
of John's Epistle. He has previously taught that if
we love our fellowmen and keep the
commandments, this will be the proof that we love
God. He now reverses this point.

> By this we know that we love the
> children of God, when we love God,
> and keep his commandments (1 John
> 5:2).

Our love of God and the keeping of his
commandments becomes the proof of our love of
fellowmen. This follows the example laid down by
the Savior. The love he bore for his Father and the
keeping of the commandment to atone, given by the
Father, became proof of his love for us. "This is the
love of God that we keep his commandments."
John continues and then adds, "...and his
commandments are not grievous." Thus the
keeping of the commandments, the love we bear for
God and Christ, and the love we bear for our
fellowmen are all interrelated. I cannot have one
and not the others. Either way one looks at it, the
principles remain the same. The principles of
obedience, love of God, and love of fellowmen share
the same perfect unity of oneness as do the Father
and Son. All these truths are comprehended as an
inseparable whole. Nor can one be eliminated and
not the others.

John then teaches that all these truths hinge on the one great truth of which he testifies—the Atonement of Christ and rebirth through that Atonement by water, blood and the spirit; the water of baptism, the atoning blood that cleanses, and the spirit that testifies and sanctifies. To possess the love that John describes, and to keep the commandments becomes proof that one is "born of God." As John taught earlier, "Everyone that loveth is born of God." This birth is spoken of in the remaining verses of the Epistle. We now know the specifics of that birth and how deeply they are intertwined with love.

Our rebirth through love and the Atonement provides the means of overcoming the world. Just prior to his Atonement, John recorded Christ telling his disciples, "Be of good cheer; I have overcome the world." The promise is now extended to the true believers that they too can overcome the world. To love, and be born again through the Savior, to "overcome the world" leads to receiving eternal life. John promises, "this is the record, that God hath given to us eternal life, and this life is in his Son. He that hath the Son hath life." John has explained to us throughout the Epistle what it truly means to have the Son. He has written his Epistle describing a true believer in Christ "that (they) may know that (they) have eternal life." Thus his Epistle becomes both an exhortation and a comfort, an exhortation to those who do not love sufficiently and a comfort to those who do.

Taken as a whole, this Epistle becomes a commentary on the Gospel of John. In it the great truths demonstrated in the gospel are magnified

and stressed. They should be studied and read
together. Both of them constitute John's testimony
of Christ. Through their testimony we understand
the power that lies behind the Atonement, the
power that makes men Christlike, and thus one
with the Father and Son.

The Second and Third Epistles of John do not
require much commentary. One is written to "the
elect lady and her children." In all probability this
is referring to the Church and her members. The
other Epistle is written to a man named Gaius. In
both we see the coming apostasy, just as John
taught us in the First Epistle.

2 JOHN

The Second Epistle follows the themes set
down in the First Epistle. John reminds "the elect
lady" of the "new commandment which we had
from the beginning that we love one another."
Sincere obedience to this commandment can be a
force to offset the growing influence of the "many
deceivers" who are denying their testimony of
Christ. John warns the Church to "look to
yourselves" in order to not "lose those things which
we have wrought." John reiterates the unity with
the Father and the Son that is promised to those
"that abide in the doctrine of Christ." There is more
John would tell the Church but prefers not to "write
with paper and ink." He expresses the hope of
being able to communicate with them face to face
and closes his Epistle.

3 JOHN

In the Third Epistle we read a beautiful statement by John that is evidence of his own deep love for the church members. He first expressed his joy at hearing of the faithfulness of Gaius, then extends that joy to include "my children" or the members of the Church.

> I have no greater joy than to
> hear that my children walk in truth
> (3 John 1:4).

We are then given a contrast of two attitudes belonging to various members of the Church. Gaius' "charity before the church" in caring for the wants and needs of those who are spreading the gospel is commended. By comparison, Diotrephes is condemned for his pride, ("...who loveth to have the pre–eminence among them,") and "malicious words." In addition to this, John relates other problems the Church is experiencing with Diotrephes, "...and not content therewith, neither doth he himself receive the brethren, and forbiddeth them that would, and casteth them out of the Church." This is an obvious example of one who is not obeying the "new commandment." He is also rejecting the authority of an Apostle. He is, therefore, in a state of apostasy even though he claims "pre–eminence among them." His lack of true charity is the evidence of his apostasy.

The comparison of Gaius and Diotrephes is followed with a warning. "Follow not that which is evil, but that which is good...he that doeth evil hath not seen God." As in most instances of John's use of seeing, this final one refers to a spiritual vision or understanding of God's will. Diotrephes, though he claims "pre–eminence" and knowledge, does not see the truth, is not filled with charity, and is therefore evil. The Church should not follow him as he will lead them into a state of apostasy.

One of the signs of a true shepherd is his love for the sheep. This Christ taught forcefully in John chapter ten. The Third Epistle has given us an example of a false shepherd. Lack of love becomes a key in his detection. John concludes his Epistle once again with the desire to speak with them "face to face" instead of writing with ink and pen.

It should be pointed out at this time that the technique of comparison shown in this small Epistle is frequently used by John. In the First Epistle light and darkness is contrasted as is love and hate, the world and the Church, the anti–Christ and the true disciple, etc. In John's Gospel we saw it forcefully used in the comparison of Nicodemus and the Samaritan woman at the well, and in the dialogues between the man born blind, who now sees, and the leaders who are in truth blind, though they claim to see. It is used in a broader way throughout the Gospel of John as we constantly see the perfidy, prejudices and intolerance of the Jewish leaders contrasted with the openness, acceptance, and love of Jesus and the disciples.

The use of contrast and comparison by John is masterfully achieved in the Revelation and it becomes the dominant theme, providing a key to its understanding. Let us now turn to the Revelation,

keeping in mind the comparative theme used so
frequently by the Apostle, John.

CHAPTER SIX

The Revelation

Kingdom of the Lamb — Kingdom of the Dragon

Up to this point we have used a chapter by chapter approach to understand John's purposes and testimony. This seemed to be an effective manner for bringing the most light to bear on the themes John stresses. In discussing Revelation another approach will be used. Rather than giving a detailed chapter by chapter interpretation, which is nearly impossible, we will look at the Revelation's images. Revelation is a book composed of successive and repeated images, allusions, and metaphors. It is John's symbolic masterpiece. We concluded the section on the three Epistles talking about comparative display as it is used by John. Rather than using a chapter by chapter approach we will use a comparative approach as we discuss the imagery in Revelation and seek for the power behind the imagery.

No one who seriously reads the New Testament can fail to recognize the literal, not symbolical, reality of a "dark power" in the world. For many Christians this produces problems. What is the origin of this evil power? Critics ask: "Why would a wise, kind, and all good Father create evil?" Dualism is one answer to this dilemma, i.e., God did not create this evil, it has always existed as an eternal opposite to God. It is as much a "first cause" as is God. Therefore the war between good and evil is a war of two independent powers. This explanation produces a myriad of problems, that, if followed to a logical and cogent end, could destroy all judgments of value. Those problems are too extensive to be treated in a commentary of this nature.

Another view of good and evil, more scriptural and without the obvious philosophical problems, states that the war is a revolution, a rebellion against the original good. It claims that evil is a parasite, there is nothing original about it. Satan, evil's advocate, is a fallen son of God in a state of perpetual rebellion. Good has "necessary existence," but evil's existence is contingent. Evil is eternal only because agency and goodness are eternal. Satan does not pursue some self–existent concept called evil, rather he seeks to pervert the good. This perversion is what we call evil. Satan is like an empty vessel. God is like a cup that is running over. This makes Satan, basically, a noncreative individual. He can twist originally good impulses and desires, or cause men to pursue good things in the wrong way. His power is in distortion. Let me simply refer to this with an image we are all familiar with. It will be helpful in understanding the context of the Revelation.

A Key to the Interpretation of Revelation

As children we have all stood in front of the curved mirrors in fun houses. The mirror reflects back an imperfect, distorted image, often barely recognizable. Satan's domain, his laws, principles, organization and authority are like a curved mirror placed beside that of God's kingdom. Darkly and imperfectly it twists with distorted mimicry the pure truths, principles, authority, and organizations of the gospel.

This concept when applied to John's Revelation provides a key to its interpretation and application. The Revelation of John flows wonderfully from image to image much like a poem. Using images, John describes and symbolically details Christ's kingdom, personality and will for mankind. He also uses imagery and symbolism to describe the adversary's kingdom, personality and will. The imagery used for Satan's kingdom is a distorted reflection coming from a curved mirror, a mirror placed in front of the imagery of Christ's kingdom. Both have keys, seals, horns, cities, brides, etc. Side by side, one after another, John places his symbols. An understanding of one symbolic image opens the mind to an understanding and application of both. They run parallel to each other, an entire masterpiece of symbolic prophecy laid down in the language of imagery showing the differences between the two kingdoms and the results of choosing to follow one or the other. The choice consists of Christ's reality or Satan's reality. It is a battle over the right to rule the earth and mankind.

Revelation draws up the battle lines covering the history of the earth and predicting the final victory. Since that battle has ever raged, Revelation has meaning for all times. We must be careful not to limit it to a single focus. With this in mind an examination of the Revelation can proceed.

The Messages to the Seven Churches

Why did John use this parallel or distorted mirror imagery? Humanity in all ages has been confronted with the choice between the forces of good and the parasitic force of evil. John knew that in the last days the choice would be magnified even greater. In terms of his own day, the seven churches of Asia faced with the choice of the reality or the twisted image, were encountering many difficulties. As we read John's specific comments to each church it becomes apparent that some were seeking the darker reflection, not the literal presence, of Christ's kingdom. With this in mind, we see that Revelation follows a pattern with the various churches. First, John compliments them on those areas of goodness they are seeking (their choice of the presence instead of the reflection). Second, he confronts, warns them and corrects their acceptance of evil (their choice of the dark reflection instead of the presence). Third, comes a promise for those "with ears to hear," which serves as a reminder of that which they will receive if they continue faithfully (the promise of the presence for eternity).

To Ephesus he writes: "I know thy works, and thy labour and thy patience..." (Revelation

2:2)—the compliment. "Nevertheless, I have somewhat against thee, because thou hast left thy first love" (Revelation 2:4)—the warning. "To him that overcometh will I give to eat of the tree of life, which is in the midst of the paradise of God" (Revelation 2:7)—the promise.

This pattern is followed with almost perfect consistency for all other churches. To Pergamos, a few verses later, John writes: "...Thou holdest fast my name, and hast not denied my faith..." (Revelation 2:13)—the compliment. "But I have a few things against thee, because thou hast there them that hold the doctrine of Balaam..." (Revelation 2:14)—the warning. "To him that overcometh will I give to eat of the hidden manna..." (Revelation 2:17)—the promise. Lest one think there is neutral ground between the two kingdoms, the message to the Laodiceans is given last of all. It breaks the pattern. John writes:

> I know thy works, that thou art neither cold nor hot: I would thou wert cold or hot.
> So then because thou art lukewarm...I will spue thee out of my mouth (Revelation 3:15–16).

Eventually one must choose. In not choosing Christ's kingdom one is choosing the adversary's.

With his individual messages to each church over, John details on a grander scale the two kingdoms, ending with a beautiful description of the eternal reward of those who "overcome." Thus the whole book, following the pattern established in the first three chapters, becomes a letter to all believers of all times, especially to those in the "latter days."

Stars, Keys, Swords—the First Images

Let us now examine the book, image by image. The first image we are introduced to in Revelation is one of dignity and beauty. It is set in chapter one as a prelude to the messages for the churches and as a constant reminder throughout the Revelation that Christ is to be worshipped not only because he is a victorious God of power, but because he is a God of love, mercy and tenderness. In a sense we could say: "If Christ were stripped of all his power we would still worship him with all our hearts and might. We would still owe him all our allegiance because of the godliness of his life, teachings and character." We not only worship Christ because he is a God, but because of the type of God he is.

Throughout the writings of John we have seen that love is the principle attribute of God. John now presents us with a visual image exemplifing that love. He describes the Savior as standing "in the midst of the seven candlesticks" (Revelation 1:13). The candlesticks (or lampstands) we are told in verse twenty, represent the seven churches of Asia. The symbol of a candlestick is fitting as an image of the Church. The Church holds the light of Christ. As a candlestick does not produce light rather it holds it up, so the Church does not shed its own light but holds up the Savior's. Neither a

candlestick nor the Church produce their own
light.

The candlestick was also symbolic of the
covenant people. They were to be the light of the
world. To the Jewish people of John's time, the
candlestick was especially significant as a
seven–branched one sat in the temple and was one
of their holiest objects.

Where does John see Christ standing in
relation to the candlesticks or churches? He is "in
the midst" of them. The image indicates that
Christ is not an absentee Lord. He is always "in the
midst" of his people. He is present. As Enoch
describes in Moses seven, when speaking to the
Lord, "Thou art *there* and thy bosom is there"
(Moses 7:30). Christ is always "*there*." He is never
truly absent from his Church.

After portraying this truth, John describes
the beauty of the Savior's appearance. He then adds
the following to his image. "And he had in his
right hand seven stars..." (Revelation 1:16). We are
told in the Joseph Smith Translation that these
stars represent the seven servants who lead the
churches. These leaders Christ holds in his right
hand in a gesture of love and guidance. Put
together we see the Savior as a God who stands with
his people (in their midst) holding his leaders in his
hand.

The star image is seen later. In chapter two,
verse twenty–eight, Christ himself is described as
"the morningstar." It is repeated in Revelation
twenty–two, verse sixteen. "I am the root and
offspring of David, and the bright and morning
star." As "the morning" or brightest star he gives

light to those he holds "in his right hand." This view of the Savior as a light giver was strongly taught in John's Gospel. It is also detailed symbolically in Abraham chapter three. There Christ is compared to a great star giving light and order to lesser stars who in turn give light to those below them. As in Revelation, the Abraham account is explaining the relationship of Christ to his prophets and people.

Out of Christ's mouth John sees "a sharp two–edged sword" (Revelation 1:16). The image of the sword is repeated in chapter nineteen, verses fifteen and twenty–one. The Joseph Smith Translation clarifies the image, so we understand it represents Christ's word, his gospel, and that it will "rule the nations" and "slay the wicked." A sword is sharp and penetrating as is Christ's word. It can cut through all falsehoods, deceptions and lies.

The total image of Christ in his earthly kingdom is completed by comparing him to "the sun shining in his strength" (Revelation 1:16) and Christ's declaration that though "dead...I am alive for evermore and have the keys of hell and of death" (Revelation 1:18).

The "key" image is interesting. In chapter three, verse seven, we are told Christ has the "Key of David." What will he do with this key? He tells us in verse eight. "I have set before thee an open door and no man can shut it...." The doors to hell and death are opened and the door to the throne and presence of his Father, described in chapter four, are opened.

Putting all these images together we see the Savior as a being of intense light, standing in the midst of his people, guiding their leaders while teaching his gospel and opening the doors to freedom and eternal life. These various images repeat throughout the Revelation. Some of them we will look at later in more detail.

Satan a Fallen Star—Counter Image

Now we will look at Satan's presence by comparison. A good look at him comes in chapter nine. There we see Satan as "a star" who "falls from heaven unto the earth" (Revelation 9:1). A few verses previous to this declaration we read of the fall of "a great star from heaven...called wormwood." It is a star bringing destruction upon the water. Christ is a bright star bringing light and life. Satan is an extinguished, fallen star, bringing death and destruction.

The star image continues in chapter twelve. Here Satan's premortal followers are described as stars. Satan is seen in this chapter as a red dragon.

His tail drew the third part of the
stars of heaven, and did cast them to
the earth (Revelation 12:4).

Instead of upholding them, as Christ does, Satan's "stars" or servants are cast down to the earth. By contrast in chapter four, verse five, we read of the final destiny of Christ's seven stars. Now described as "lamps of fire burning," they are "before the throne," having been lifted up. As Satan is a fallen

star, so his followers are also fallen. Their light is
extinguished. They offer no guidance.

Returning to chapter nine, verse one, we read
that Satan also holds a key: "to him was given the
key of the bottomless pit." Ironically it is also a key
to hell, just as Christ holds. Also ironic is the first
verse in chapter twenty where an angel, "having
the key of the bottomless pit," locks Satan in his own
hell for a thousand years. But until that day, Satan
holds the key to his own type of hell. Instead of
releasing prisoners from captivity, which John
promises Christ will do, Satan unleashes a plague
of locusts to torment men for a season of five
months. Described in military language, this
plague of locusts can parallel Christ's candlesticks
or followers and later parallel the army that
accompanies his Second Coming. They bring the
darkness of smoke which obscures "the sun and the
air" rather than bringing light. Christ stands "in
the midst" of candlesticks with a countenance like
the sun. Satan stands as "a king" in the midst of
his army of locusts darkening the sun and the
whole world.

Later in chapter twenty–one Christ becomes
a light greater then the sun for those who have
received his reward. "And the city had no need of
the sun, neither of the moon, to shine in it: for the
glory of God did lighten it, and the Lamb is the light
thereof" (Revelation 21:23). This description
continues in the following chapter. We read:

> And there shall be no night
> there; and they need no candle, neither
> light of the sun; for the Lord God giveth

them light: and they shall reign for
ever and ever (Revelation 22:5).

Christ can eclipse the sun with his glory. Satan
can only "darken" it with the smoke of his evil
influences and his destructive wars.

The "smoke" ascending out of hell in chapter
nine represents another parallel image seen
earlier. In chapter eight we read:

> And another angel came and
> stood at the altar, having a golden
> censer; and there was given unto him
> much incense, that he should offer it
> with the prayers of all saints upon the
> golden altar which was before the
> throne.
> And the smoke of the incense,
> which came with the prayers of the
> saints, ascended up before God out of
> the angel's hand (Revelation 8:3–4).

Sweet smelling incense representing the prayers
and desires of the saints are contrasted with the
foul, choking, plague–ridden smoke of Satan.
Satan's smoke, represents the "plagues," desire,
and influences of the devil and his followers. It is
the smoke of war, evil, and destruction. It
contributes to the blindness of the people.

The Lamb—the Dragon
Central Images

In the first chapter Christ declared that he died and was alive again. John presents us with an image for this declaration in chapter five, verse six.

> I beheld...in the midst of the elders, stood a Lamb as it had been slain, having twelve horns and twelve eyes which are the twelve servants of God sent forth into all the earth (Revelation 5:6 JST).

Five verses later, those who Christ made "kings and priests" praise him for his Atoning sacrifice and Resurrection by saying:

> ...Worthy is the Lamb that was slain to receive power, and riches, and wisdom, and strength, and honour, and glory, and blessings (Revelation 5:12).

Now look at the distorted image of the slain lamb. Opposite the slain lamb with twelve horns we have "a great red dragon, having seven heads and ten horns, and seven crowns upon his heads" (Revelation 12:3). His red color could be parallel to Christ's appearing in red clothing at the Second Coming."And he (Christ) was clothed with a vesture dipped in blood" (Revelation 19:13). This signifies his having "treadeth in the wine–vat" as we read in the Doctrine and Covenants.

And I have trampled them in my
fury, and I did tread upon them in
mine anger, and their blood have I
sprinkled upon my garments, and
stained all my raiment; for this was
the day of vengeance which was in my
heart (D&C 133:51).

Red is also an appropriate color for the
dragon. However in his case, the redness could
symbolize his immersion in sin and death and his
glorying in it.

The dragon also has many horns. The twelve
horns of the slain lamb represent the twelve
Apostles who bear his authority or priesthood on the
earth. The horns of the dragon represent Satan's
ambassadors who wield his authority, an authority
of power, money and the things of the world, as we
shall see in chapters sixteen through eighteen. The
twelve apostles go "forth into all the earth" and find
followers of the Lamb, exalting them into "a great
multitude which no man could number, of all
nations, kindreds, and people, and tongues..."
(Revelation 7:9). Satan's domains also have
"power...over all kindreds and tongues and
nations" (Revelation 13:7). In chapter seventeen
Satan is seen exercising power over "peoples, and
multitudes, and nations, and tongues" (Revelation
17:15).

We might pause here and examine the
appropriateness of a seven—headed dragon and
later the seven—headed beast. Satan's kingdom
has many heads and many offensives. Some come
from deceptive and apostate religions, some from

political, economic, scientific and social falsehoods. God's kingdom does not have such confusion. This was brought out in the First Epistle in the discussion of the anti–Christ. There is one Godhead united in purpose, deed, love, etc., a single head. Satan's kingdom presents confusion.

It would be foolish indeed to single out one head and say, "Viola, l'enemie" and ignore the other six. The seven heads may also stand for different aspects of Satan's kingdom during different periods of the earth's history. There are seven dispensations. There has been a "head". Satan does not give up, but finds ways to probe men's weaknesses in every age and time. He will even destroy the peace of the Millennium near the close of the one thousand years.

The dragon image is therefore, powerful in presenting two aspects of Satan's kingdom as opposed to Christ's, that of confusion and multiplicity against unity and order. Also like the Hydra in the myth of Hercules, the severing of a head may not result in its death but breed more and more evil. Such is the nature of the adversary.

As is seen in the Book of Mormon in the case of Korihor and the trampling Zoramites, one head may even seek to destroy another. Both represented anti–Christs. When Korihor was no longer useful, Satan's next power (the Zoramites) killed him, bringing from Mormon the commentary that Satan will not uphold his servants (Alma 30:60). We saw already that Christ does.

In Revelation, this self–destructing mode of Satanic inspiration is also followed. Chapter seventeen commences with the "whore," the great and abominable church, sitting upon a scarlet beast in a compatible relationship, upholding and supporting each other. At the end of the chapter we read:

> And the ten horns which thou sawest upon the beast, these shall hate the whore, and shall make her desolate and naked, and shall eat her flesh, and burn her with fire (Revelation 17:16).

Christ, the "slain lamb" declares that he was dead and is now alive. This represents his greatest miracle and the main reason the saints "worshipped him that liveth, forever and ever" (Rev. 5:14). Satan's seven—headed beast makes the same claim of resurrection.

> And I saw one of his heads as it were wounded to death; and his deadly wound was healed: and all the world wondered after the beast (Revelation 13:3).

Without making a specific interpretation we can still find power, application and meaning here. Satan's kingdom is such that part of it may fall for a time, seemingly destroyed, but it will soon rise up again, perhaps more malevolent than ever. He constantly makes the claim that there are none who are able to defeat him or make him afraid. His kingdom will go on and on. Thus he claims that the eternal nature of Christ's kingdom will be applied to him.

Because of this great "wonder" the world "worshipped the beast, saying, Who is like unto the beast? who is able to make war with him?" (Revelation 13:4). Thus mankind gave honor to "a beast" instead of "the lamb." This explains why the "name of blasphemy" is on the seven heads. Anything or anyone who claims the worship due the Savior is not only in a state of rebellion, but also in a state of blasphemy.

Later in chapter thirteen we see the image of another beast who has "two horns like a lamb, and he spake as a dragon." Again the claim "like a lamb" has significance. This new creature promulgates the worship of "the first beast, whose deadly wound was healed" (Revelation 13:12). He commands the making of "an image to the beast, which had the wound by a sword and did live" (Revelation 13:14). It is this worship that stirs the giving of a mark to its adherents, but that will be discussed later.

The worshipful praise of the people "who's able to make war with him" may provide a clue to the seven—headed beast. It is a reference to power in a worldly way with an emphasis on war. Given the nature of war in Revelation, we should probably not look for religious meaning in the healing of the wounded head. Rather we should look for a political or a "ruling" interpretation in terms of power and ability to control numerous people. Throughout the history of the world we have seen numerous kingdoms, or "beasts," patterned after Satan's principles, ruling the world. We have given them different names from Babylon to Rome, but the resultant misery and slavery for mankind

remains the same. Before we get carried away,
though, in specific interpretations, let us remember
John's imagery is difficult to pinpoint, but taken in
a broader sense can have multiple applications.

Satan's claims to many kingdoms, powers,
dominions, etc., are seen in the wearing of multiple
crowns both on the dragon of chapter twelve and on
the beast of chapter thirteen and adds significance
to the statement, "Who is able to make war with
him?" These kingdoms he once offered to the Savior
as a temptation. Christ, however, when he comes
in glory, is seen wearing "on his head...many
crowns" (Revelation 19:12) signifying that he is the
true ruler of heaven and earth. It is significant that
in chapter four, verse ten:

> ...four and twenty elders fall
> down before him that sat on the throne
> (of God) and worship him that liveth
> for ever and ever, and *cast their*
> *crowns before the throne* saying,
> Thou art worthy, O Lord, to
> receive glory and honour and power...
> (Revelation 4:10–11).

The elders recognize that only the Lord is worthy to
wear "many crowns" and they render their own
crowns of glory to God in humble gratitude and
praise.

"Out of the Mouth"

We saw earlier a sword preceding out of the
mouth of the Savior. The sword is God's word, his

gospel. With it he slays the wicked in two ways: (1.) They repent when they hear his gospel taught; and, (2.) they are judged and condemned by the Lord for their wickedness. Repentance and forgiveness through the Atonement is the better of the two ways of "slaying" the wicked with the word.

What comes "out of the mouth" of Satan and his beasts? Let us see. In chapter sixteen the seven angels pour out their vials upon the earth. These are then symbolically represented by allusions to the plagues of Egypt. (Much of Revelation imagery can be traced to the Old Testament.) Alluding to the plague of frogs, John states:

> And I saw three unclean spirits like frogs come out of the mouth of the dragon, and out of the mouth of the beast, and out of the mouth of the false prophet.
>
> For they are the spirits of devils, working miracles, which go forth unto the kings of the earth and of the whole world, to gather them to the battle of that great day of God Almighty (Revelation 16:13–14).

The sword that comes from the Savior is a discerning and penetrating sword that divides good and evil, right and wrong, truth and falsehood. It is a sword of truth. It brings life through truth and repentance, even though it may also bring destruction through judgment. The gospel brings peace and unity through repentance and pure principles. Satan's frogs are deceivers. The frogs

bring the war and destruction of "Armageddon."
The gospel proclaims that peace comes through
surrender to Christ. The frogs "deceive" by
proclaiming peace comes through conquest. But as
John taught earlier in the Revelation, "He that
killeth with the sword must be killed with the
sword." The irony of this verse is easily seen when
taken in the context of the entire Revelation.
Summarizing this aspect of the comparison of what
comes out of the mouth of Christ and what comes
from Satan's, we would say truth is contrasted with
lies. This we would expect, for as Christ has been a
God of truth from the beginning, so Satan has been
a "liar from the beginning," the "father of all lies."
      In chapter twelve John uses another image of
what comes out of Satan's mouth:

>   And the serpent cast out of his
> mouth water as a flood after the
> woman, that he might cause her to be
> carried away of the flood (Revelation
> 12:15).

The image is one of a filthy outpouring of water sent
to drown the Church and its efforts to establish the
kingdom of God. The Church seeks by "the word"
or sword of Christ to bring the kingdom of God to
fruition. If the sword is the gospel, as we have
seen, the flood must be, like the smoke of the pit, the
evil influences, teachings, philosophies, sins, etc. of
the world. Since Satan is the father of lies, lies
come from his mouth as a flood. These are sent to
deceive the Church. All these are thrown at the
saints. At times this tactic of Satan is successful as

it "drives the woman into the wilderness" of
apostasy which comes by compromising the purity
of Christ's living water with the filth of Satan's
flood.

This flood of filthy water is but another
distortion of the virtue that Christ offers. At the end
of the Revelation, John sees the celestial glory of
God. He is shown "a pure river of water of life,
clear as crystal, proceeding out of the throne of God
and of the Lamb." Christ's water is "pure." It
brings life, not death by drowning. It is "clear" not
foul. It waters the tree of life whose "leaves of the
tree were for the healing of the nations" (Revelation
22:1–2). That water should never be compromised
with the flood from Satan's mouth.

There are other mirrored images that need to
be included as we discuss "out of the mouth." The
two witnesses that testify in the streets of Jerusalem
are described in the following manner:

> These are the two olive trees, and
> the two candlesticks standing before
> the God of the earth.
> And if any man will hurt them,
> fire proceedeth *out of their mouth*, and
> devoureth their enemies: and if any
> man will hurt them, he must in this
> manner be killed.
> These have power to shut
> heaven, that it rain not in the days of
> their prophecy: and have power over
> waters to turn them to blood, and to
> smite the earth with all plagues, as
> often as they will (Revelation 11:4–6).

John uses a considerable amount of allusion to the Old Testament. This is an example of that literary technique. Elijah and Moses are two of the greatest Old Testament prophets. The description of the two witnesses follows a close parallel to the prophetic miracles of Elijah and Moses. Fire does not literally proceed from the mouths of the two witnesses, but they come in the spirit and authority of Moses and Elijah. They come to reveal the true God of the earth. His power is superior to the adversary's as Moses proved Jehovah was greater than the gods of Egypt, and Elijah showed that Jehovah was more powerful then Baal. The witnesses speak with the same priesthood authority and are obeyed. That authority is superior to the world. Both Moses and Elijah's missions involved helping their people to choose between the gods of the world or the true God of heaven. This is ever the mission of Christ's witnesses.

In chapter nine the sixth angel looses four angels "bound in the bottomless pit" (Revalation 9:14 JST). They go forth described as the great army of horsemen to "slay the third part of men." As they go forth to slay, "out of their mouth's issued fire and smoke and brimstone" (Revelation 9:17).

This prophecy could be interpreted literally or figuratively. If Satan's army of horsemen is a symbolic representation of a modern army, fire and destruction coming from modern weapons, such as tanks or cannons, would fulfill John's description. If we compare it to the meaning of the fire from the mouths of the two witnesses, then the fulfillment could come as the army orders the destructions, calling upon the authority of temporal powers with which Satan rules the earth.

Horses and Horsemen

This image of Satan's army of horsemen destroying with fire coming from their mouths, is the distorted reflection of yet another of John's images. John tells us that "the number of the army of the horsemen (Satan's) were two hundred thousand thousand" (Revelation 9:16). He also sees "them that sat on them" (Revelation 9:17). In chapter nineteen John introduces us to another army or horsemen—that which belongs to Christ as he comes in triumph.

> And I saw heaven opened, and behold a white horse; and he that sat upon him was called Faithful and True, and in righteousness he doth judge and make war.
>
> His eyes were as a flame of fire, and on his head were many crowns; and he had a name written, that no man knew, but he himself.
>
> And he was clothed with a vesture dipped in blood: and his name is called The Word of God.
>
> And the armies which were in heaven followed him upon white horses, clothed in fine linen, white and clean.
>
> And out of his mouth goeth a sharp sword, that with it he should

> smite the nations: and he shall rule
> them with a rod of iron: and he
> treadeth the winepress of the
> fierceness and wrath of Almighty God
> (Revelation 19:11–15).

This scripture ties many images together including
those dealing with "out of his mouth." Satan's
army brings destruction but Christ conquers it and
slays "the remnant" with his sword. This is the
prelude to the millennial reign and establishment
of the New Jerusalem. We can also compare
Christ's first "triumphal entry" into Jerusalem
prior to his Atonement with this second "triumph."
The first time he rode a donkey, symbolic of
humility. The second time he comes on a horse, the
ancient symbol of power and war. The first time he
conquered Satan with his humble submission to his
Father's will. The second appearance will cast
Satan out and establish his millennial reign.

Horses are used elsewhere in the Revelation
as symbols and images. In the sixth chapter the
opening of the seals reveals four horses. The first,
as is seen in chapter nineteen, is a white horse. Its
rider, often interpreted as Enoch, has a crown, a
bow and conquers. If Enoch is the correct
interpretation, his conquering evil and Satan by
establishing Zion is a type or foreshadow of what
Christ will do when he comes riding a white horse
to conquer, and like Enoch, he will establish a
millennial Zion society. However, it is the other
horsemen that provide strong parallel images.

The opening of the second through fifth seals
bring to light some interesting parallels with the

final conquest of Christ's mounted army, and his establishment of the millennial era. Joseph Smith tells us in section seventy–seven of the Doctrine and Covenants that the opening of the seals represents thousand year periods of the earth's history. The history of the world during the period of these seals has largely been ruled by Satan with blood and horror. The red, black and pale horsemen are his.

The red horseman takes *peace* from the earth. This is normally interpreted as the generation of the flood, where men were so wicked and self–destructive through war and hatred that God destroyed them all, saving only Noah and his family.

The black horseman carries "a pair of balances" bringing famine, and an unjust distribution of the earth's goods for which men must pay dearly. This is the generation and dispensation of Abraham, Isaac, Jacob and Joseph. There were great famines on the earth during this time which are related in the Old Testament.

The pale horse brings "death and hell." This is the period of successive conquests by each new rising power. Assyria, Babylon, Persia, Greece, Rome, etc., all in turn brought misery to mankind as they ruled the earth with blood and horror.

The fifth seal brings martyrdom for the saints. This is the dispensation of Christ. It is filled with martyrdom from John the Baptist, the Savior, his Apostles and disciples, to the thousands of Christians persecuted throughout the Dark Ages in the inter–Christian wars and Reformation.

The opening of the above seals shows clearly the manner in which Satan rules the earth through

his minsters of power. He brings war, famine,
death, violence, martyrdom, and misery. Contrast
this "ruling" of the world by Satan with what
Christ, mounted on his white horse brings. In the
last chapters of Revelation the Savior brings peace,
judgment and plenty, conquers death and hell and
resurrects the "souls of them that were beheaded
for the witness of Jesus" (Revelation 20:4). In
summation John teaches that "God shall wipe
away all tears from their eyes; and there shall be no
more death, neither sorrow, nor crying, neither
shall there be any more pain: for the former things
are passed away" (Revelation 21:4). The old
horsemen have been defeated by the conquering
return of the Savior, mounted on a white horse.

Names, Seals, Marks

Some will be privileged to ride triumphant
with Christ's army.

> And they shall see his face; and
> his name shall be in their foreheads
> (Revelation 22:4).

Those who have the Savior's name in their
foreheads ride with the triumphant Christ. The
name in the forehead represents one of the major
parallel images in the Revelation. Let us seek to
understand it. We are first introduced to it in
chapter three. The letter to the Saints in
Philadelphia includes the following promise:

> ...I will write upon him the
> name of my God, and the name of the
> city of my God, which is new
> Jerusalem...and I will write upon him
> my new name (Revelation 3:12).

This promise is fulfilled in chapter nineteen with
the description of Christ's army and in chapter
twenty–two quoted above. It is also fulfilled in the
first verse of chapter fourteen. John sees "the
lamb" standing on mount Zion, "and with him an
hundred forty and four thousand, having his
Father's name written in their foreheads
(Revelation 14:1).

Chapter seven, however, gives us the leading
image of God's name being written in the foreheads
of his followers. Before the four angels at the
corners of the earth are loosed, a fifth angel ascends
from the east "having the seal of the living God."
He delays the four destroying angels until he has
had time to seal "the servants of our God in their
foreheads" (Revelation 7:2–3). We are then given
the number (144,000) of the sealed. Following this
"a great multitude, which no man could number, of
all nations" is sealed. Joseph Smith explained this
passage of sealing by teaching "it signifies sealing
the blessings upon their heads, meaning the
everlasting covenants, thereby making their calling
and election sure" (*Teachings of the Prophet Joseph
Smith*, p. 321). In the Doctrine and Covenants,
section seventy–seven, we learn the 144,000 are
high priests "ordained unto the holy order of God, to
administer the everlasting gospel...to bring as
many as will come (the great multitude) to the

church of the Firstborn" (D&C 77:11).   John
continues his description of those who are sealed
and carry God's name in their foreheads.

> These are they which came out
> of great tribulation and have washed
> their robes, and made them white in
> the blood of the Lamb.
> ...and serve him [God] day and
> night in his temple (Revelation
> 7:14–15).

The seal and name denote ownership. These high
priests belong to Christ. They bear his mark or
brand, and they hold his authority or priesthood or
sealing. They are his servants or, as he prefers,
"his friends." Alma refers to a similar image when
he asked the Saints of Zarahemla: "Have ye
spiritually been born of God? *Have ye received his
image in your countenances?*" (Alma 5:14). When a
man joins the church through baptism he signifies
he has been born again. He becomes a "son or
daughter" of Christ. He promises to "grow–up" to
be like the father of his rebirth, like Christ. He does
this by taking upon himself Christ's name, by
remembering him, and by obeying his commandments. Doing this, he becomes more and more like
Christ.   He receives more covenants and
knowledge. Slowly the Savior's image is engraved
on his countenance and Christ seals the individual
his own. This we easily understand, as it is a
major theme throughout John's writing. If we
prefer, this sealing can be looked upon as a brand or

mark placed on Christ's true sheep just as we mark
or brand animals today to clarify ownership.

Further light is cast on the "sealing of the
righteous" by understanding one of the main
allusions John uses constantly throughout
Revelation. Over and over he alludes to the plagues
of Egypt and the freeing of the twelve tribes from
their captivity. John talks of:

1. "Hail and fire mingled with blood"
   (Revelation 8:7).
2. "Sea became blood" (Revelation 8:8, 16:4).
3. "Part of the sun was smitten...and was
   darkened" (Revelation 8:12).
4. "And there came...locusts upon the earth"
   (Revelation 9:3).
5. "There fell a noisome and grievous sore"
   (Revelation 16:2).
6. "Three unclean spirits like frogs"
   (Revelation 16:13).

All six of the above plagues are seen in Exodus.
They were used to humble Pharoah. There are
many such allusions to Old Testament plagues and
prophets. Those who are sealed in Revelation are
spared from the plagues. In Exodus, the final
plague was the death of the first born by the
destroying angel. But those who believed marked
their doors with lamb's blood. This symbolized the
atoning blood of the Savior, which saves mankind
from "the destroying angel" or Satan. In
Revelation, the sealing or marking of the twelve
tribes and the numberless hosts protects them from
the plagues that the angels pour out. This allusion

would suggest the sealing in Revelation also has to do with the Atonement and the protective mark Christ places on those who have accepted it. He seals them his through their faith and repentance in his atoning blood.

The Mark of the Beast

With all the preceding in mind, let's look at Satan's dark reflection. Satan's beasts are described in chapter thirteen. They are given "great authority" by the devil, just as Christ's servants and kingdom rule by his authority or priesthood. The first beast is healed of the "deadly wound" it received. The second beast inspires the worship of the first. In some of the most disputed and talked about verses in the Revelation we are told:

> And he causeth all, both small and great, rich and poor, free and bond, to receive a mark in their right hand, or in their foreheads:
> And that no man might buy or sell, save he that had the mark, or the name of the beast, or the number of his name.
> Here is wisdom. Let him that hath understanding count the number of the beast: for it is the number of a man; and his number is Six hundred threescore and six (Revelation 13:16–18).

Now what can all this mean? It cannot be given a specific interpretation at this time, especially the number. Perhaps there will come a day when we will understand. But, using the parallelism we have seen is a major thrust of John's visions, we can come to some significant understanding without knowing the detailed future fulfillment.

As we live the principles of Christ's gospel we carry his mark. Those who follow the principles of Satan's kingdom, (as represented by the beasts), it laws and its deceptions, begin to bear his mark. Satan is also called the "father" of his "children" or the "master" or his "servants." His mark in the "forehead and right hand" proclaim to all that this individual belongs to him, just as a slave's brand in the ancient world denoted ownership. Those who bear Satan's mark, in contrast to Christ's "friends," are in truth his slaves. According to John "small and great, rich and poor, free and bond" will bear the mark of Satan. His image will be engraved on their countenances also.

What are these people from all levels of society doing to make them eligible to carry his mark? We are told they "worshipped the beast" and they "worshipped the image of the beast" (Revelation 13:4, 15). We should not conclude necessarily that this worship is an overt religious act. Perhaps those who worship Satan are not aware of what they are doing, but their actions denote that they worship him just as a servant of Christ's actions show worship of the Master better than words or rituals. Remember Christ said, "I would thou wert cold or hot" (Revelation 3:15).

There is no middle ground. We are either for him or against him. King Benjamin said:

> For how knoweth a man the master whom he has not served, and who is a stranger unto him, and is far from the thoughts and intents of his heart? (Mosiah 5:13).

If the thoughts and intents of our heart are centered in Christ and his gospel, he is our master. However if our thoughts and intents are similar to those of Satan, he is our master. King Benjamin goes on to exhort the followers of Christ, those that take his name, to be:

> ...steadfast and immovable, always abounding in good works, that Christ, the Lord God Omnipotent, may seal you his, that you may be brought to heaven, that ye may have everlasting salvation and eternal life, through the wisdom, and power, and justice, and mercy of him who created all things, in heaven and in earth, who is God above all. Amen (Mosiah 5:15).

I am sealed his by my steadfastness and my good works. By contrast Satan seals me his by my evil works. Additional help is given to us by remembering John's heavy use of Old Testament imagery and practices. In Deuteronomy we read:

> Hear, O Israel: The Lord our God is one Lord:

> And thou shalt love the Lord thy
> God with all thine heart, and with all
> thy soul, and with all thy might.
> And these words, which I
> command thee this day, shall be in
> thine heart:
> And thou shalt teach them
> diligently unto thy children, and shalt
> talk of them when thou sittest in thine
> house, and when thou walkest by the
> way, and when thou liest down, and
> when thou risest up.
> And thou shalt bind them for a
> sign upon thine hand, and they shall
> be as frontlets between thine eyes
> (Deuteronomy 6:4–8).

These verses are extremely important to the Jewish
faith, both now and at the time of John. The Jews
took them literally and made phylacteries, or small
boxes, containing passages of the law of Moses
written on parchment scrolls. These they bound on
their left arm and on their forehead during
worship. However, the meaning in Deuteronomy,
aside from the literal application of the Jews,
suggests the nearness of the laws of God. The laws,
principles and teachings of the gospel should be
constantly visible—always before our eyes to guide
our actions. All we look at should be governed by
the scriptures and principles of God's laws. The
same is true of all that our hands reach for or do.
Our deeds should be governed by the laws of God.
In light of John's emphasis on love, the verse has
special application here. The law that we should

bind on our foreheads and hands is, "Thou shalt
love the Lord thy God with all thine heart, and with
all thy soul, and with all thy might."

If we use this allusion with Satan's mark on
the forehead and hand, we understand that those in
Satan's kingdom are there because they "loved" evil
with all their heart, soul and might. Their desires
and intentions and all they reached for with their
hands were governed by Satan's treasures,
principles and laws.

The Mark of Materialism

Does the worship of the beast take a specific
form with which John is concerned? Are there evil
works that cause one to be sealed or marked by him
other than the general application we just studied?
There are hints in the Revelation to direct us to
some specifics. Chapter thirteen verse seventeen
tells us that no man could "buy or sell save he that
had the mark or the name of the beast, or the
number of his name." "Buy or sell" are key words,
for among other things in Satan's arsenal, the
treasures of the earth are powerful in stirring up
men to great evil. Does not Satan rule the earth
through its treasures? Does he not say to the whole
world, "Everything in this world can be obtained
through money?" Those who live by this principle of
selfishness and greed bear the mark of Satan. The
Book of Mormon is filled with living examples of
those who fall to this reasoning and are sealed by
Satan because of their worship of the "fine things of
the world" (4 Nephi 24).

Why could one not "buy or sell?" Why would the mark be on all, rich, poor, bond, free, etc? Often the rationalization of those who do not wish to leave Satan's employ is; "What will become of us? This is the way the world is. How can you actually and practically live the gospel principles in a dog eat dog, law of the jungle world?" It must be business as usual. Korihor states this theory, sometimes called Social Darwinism, in Alma.

> And many more such things did he say unto them, telling them that there could be no more atonement made for the sins of men, but every man fared in this life according to the management of the creature; therefore every man prospered according to his genius, and that every man conquered according to his strength; and whatsoever a man did was no crime (Alma 30:17).

Materialism is one of Satan's most oft used and effective weapons. Remember the chastisement Christ gave to the Laodiceans, the only church that did not receive a compliment, those who were "neither cold nor hot." Their sin was that of materialism—the worship of wealth.

> Because thou sayest, I am rich, and increased with goods, and have need of nothing; and knowest not that thou art wretched, and miserable, and poor, and blind, and naked:

> I counsel thee to buy of me gold
> tried in the fire, that thou mayest be
> rich; and white raiment, that thou
> mayest be clothed, and that the shame
> of thy nakedness do not appear; and
> anoint thine eyes with eyesalve, that
> thou mayest see (Revelation 3:17–18).

This "mark" is very pointedly brought out in chapter eighteen dealing with the fall of Babylon. Throughout the chapter we read of great mourning by two main groups—the "kings of the earth" and "the merchants of the earth." The emphasis is on the merchants who have "waxed rich through the abundance of her delicacies" (Revelation 18:3). The Lord then immediately tells "my people" to "come out of her,...be not partakers of her sins" (Revelation 18:4). Notice the specific cause of all the mourning in chapter eighteen?

> And the merchants of the earth
> shall weep and mourn over her; for no
> man buyeth their merchandise any
> more:
> The merchandise of gold, and
> silver, and precious stones, and of
> pearls, and fine linen, and purple, and
> silk, and scarlet, and all thyine wood,
> and all manner vessels of ivory, and all
> manner vessels of most precious wood,
> and of brass, and iron, and marble,
> And cinnamon, and odours, and
> ointments, and frankincense, and
> wine, and oil, and fine flour, and

> wheat, and beasts, and sheep, and
> horses, and chariots, and slaves, and
> souls of men (Revelation 18:11–13).

This is quite an extensive list with powerful and haunting last words, "the souls of men." Jesus once asked: "For what is a man profited, if he shall gain the whole world, and lose his own soul?" (Matthew 16:26).

The emphasis on wealth continues through chapter eighteen.

> The fruits thy soul lusted after
> are departed from thee..." (Revelation
> 18:14).

> The merchants of these things
> which were made rich by her, shall
> stand afar off for the fear of her
> torment.. (Revelation 18:15).

> For in one hour so great riches is
> come to nought" (Revelation 18:17).

> Alas, alas, that great city,
> wherein were made rich all that had
> ships in the seas by reason of her
> costliness!" (Revelation 18:19).

> ...For thy merchants were the
> great men of the earth; for by thy
> *sorceries* were all nations deceived
> (Revelation 18:23).

In the last verse of chapter nine John relates that in spite of the warning judgments that are coming "neither repented [they] of their murders, nor of their *sorceries*, nor of their fornication, nor of their thefts" (Revelation 9:21). Coupling chapter eighteen with this verse we have an idea of the motive behind the sorceries, murders, fornication and theft, all of which lead to the great destructions.

The goals of a secret combination, Satan's most authoritative kingdom on earth, is power and gain. One of its principles was best stated by Cain, when he justified the "economic" murder of his brother. He said, "Am I my brother's keeper?" (Moses 5:34). After all, Cain is saying, you have to "look out for number one." Cain was the original member of the "me generation." Did not the Jaredites and Nephites find destruction in the proud money–glutted world of the Gadianton robbers and in the allurement of "costly apparel?" All these "mark" an individual and "number" him among Satan's fold to be "sealed" his at the judgment. As chapter nine indicates, "yet [they] repented not of the works of their hands" (Revelation 9:20). Their lifestyles, greed, lusts, and their thirst for power were unrestrained.

Speaking in modern terms we can find interesting insights by referring to a scripture that relates to this problem. It is given in the context of the "calamities which should come upon the inhabitants of the earth." Notice the substance of Doctrine and Covenants 1:16, especially the use of the word "image."

> They seek not the Lord to
> establish his righteousness, but every
> man walketh in his own way, and after
> the *image* of his own God, whose
> image is in the likeness of the world,
> and whose substance is that of an idol,
> which waxeth old and shall perish in
> Babylon, even Babylon the great, which
> shall fall (D&C 1:16).

President Spencer W. Kimball identified this
problem with hauntingly familiar words.

> Many people spend most of their
> time working in the service of a
> *self-image* that includes sufficient
> money, stocks, bonds, investment,
> portfolios, property, credit cards,
> furnishings, automobiles, and the like
> to guarantee carnal security
> throughout, it is hoped, a long and
> happy life (1976 June *Ensign*).

Could these warnings and the use of the word
image give us a clue to a broader interpretation of
the "image of the beast" described in chapter
thirteen, verses fourteen and fifteen?

Contrast this "buy and sell" world of Satan's
where even a man's soul is up for sale with the
Savior's kingdom. Instead of Cain's "Am I my
brother's keeper," Christ's basic principle is "let
every man esteem his brother as himself"
(D&C 38:24–35). John points out the generous
liberality of Christ's kingdom in the last chapter.

"He that overcometh shall *inherit all things...*"
(Revelation 21:7). There is no buying and selling,
but an inheritance. How is that inheritance given?
John answers: "And whosoever will, let him take
the water of life *freely*" (Revelation 22:17). Compare
the bowing before the idols of the world with
Christ's invitation in chapter three to "sit with me
in my throne" (Revelation 3:21). One of the great
teachings of avoiding Satan's mark is to think of
these promises and be satisfied with just enough to
be sufficient for our needs as Paul counseled, and to
use the material wealth with which we are blessed
to build the kingdom of God on earth.

The Mark of Militarism

There is another aspect of Satan's "mark"
that Revelation teaches us. It too is a hallmark of
Satan's kingdom—that of war, military might and
conquest. Secret combinations seek "power" along
with "gain." It is difficult to separate the two. Most
wars, if examined deeply, are fought for economic
reasons. The desire for conquest, hatred, mistrust
and greed between nations will lead, we are told
throughout Revelation, to "the battle of that great
day" (Revelation 16:14). If we want to see this
"mark" at work we need only read of the
self-destructive mode of the Nephites and
Jaredites. The "battle of that great day" will be
motivated by similar evils. The lust for power and
conquest is also the "mark of the beast." Even the
symbolic names of the two kingdoms reflect their
different camps. Christ is the lamb—meek, gentle,
innocent. Satan is a beast—ferocious, cunning and

murderous. The images are clear and their marks easily seen in the present world of the "last days." Our job is to not be part of them. Does not the sealing of Christ's sheep by their love and devotion for him and the sealing of Satan's sheep by their lusts, greed, and desire for conquest correspond perfectly with the messages of the First Epistle?

Before leaving the seal and mark of the beast, I would refer the reader to the 1976 Bicentennial issue of the *Ensign* earlier quoted. President Kimball wrote the First Presidency message entitled "The False Gods We Worship." It is insightful that therein he identifies materialism and militarism as the two main false gods of the twentieth century. Speaking of war and its causes President Kimball said:

> We are a warlike people, easily distracted from our assignment of preparing for the coming of the Lord. When enemies rise up, we commit vast resources to the fabrication of gods of stone and steel—ships, planes, missiles, fortifications—and depend on them for protection and deliverance. When threatened, we become anti-enemy instead of pro–kingdom of God; we train a man in the art of war and call him a patriot, thus, in the manner of Satan's counterfeit of true patriotism, perverting the Savior's teaching:

'Love your enemies,
bless them that curse you,
do good to them that hate
you, and pray for them
which despitefully use
you, and persecute you;
'That ye may be the
children of your Father
which is in heaven'
(Matthew 5:44–45).

We forget that if we are
righteous the Lord will either not
suffer our enemies to come upon
us—and this is the special promise to
the inhabitants of the land of the
Americas (see 2 Nephi. 1:7)—or he will
fight our battles for us (Exodus 14:14;
D&C 98:37, to name only two references
of many).

What are we to fear when the
Lord is with us? Can we not take the
Lord at his word and exercise a
particle of faith in him? Our
assignment is affirmative: to forsake
the things of the world as ends in
themselves: to leave off idolatry and
press forward in faith: to carry the
gospel to our enemies, that they might
no longer be our enemies.

We must leave off the worship of
modern–day idols and a reliance on
the 'arm of flesh,' for the Lord has said
to all the world in our day, "I will not

spare any that remain in Babylon"
(D&C 64:24).

The Great Gatherings to the Feast

Materialism and militaristic conquest, two
mainstays of Satan's kingdom, will cause a
gathering to take place. Once again we have a
distorted image of the gathering of the elect in the
last days. The unclean "frog" spirits that proceeded
out of the mouth of the dragon, beast, and false
prophets, "go forth unto the kings of the whole
world, to gather them to the battle of that great day
of God Almighty...And he gathered them together
into a place called in the Hebrew tongue
Armageddon" (Revelation 16:14, 16). Later we read
this gathering will also be a feast, a "supper of the
great God" (Revelation 19:17). Ironically, however,
those who come to feast, are the main course. An
angel calls for "all the fouls that fly" to come to the
feast.

> That ye may eat the flesh of
> kings, and the flesh of captains, and
> the flesh of mighty men, and the flesh
> of horses, and of them that sit on them,
> and the flesh of all men, both free and
> bond, both small and great
> (Revelation 19:18).

There is a powerful ironic image being used here
that we will miss if we do not read carefully. In the
preceding chapter Babylon is described as, "the hold
of every foul spirit, and a cage of every unclean and

hateful bird" (Revelation 18:2). The "unclean and hateful birds" of prey—the carrion hunters, the warmongers and the powerful that the world has admired and caged like would—be songbirds, will be let loose on their masters. Indeed the very masters unlock the cages. With justified irony they become the victims of their own sins and malignancies. Remember that John earlier stated, "He that killeth with the sword must be killed with the sword" (Revelation 13:10). We see this literal self-destruction in both the Nephite and Jaredite societies. John saw the destruction of his own people and the temple through the military messiahs who revolted against Rome and brought their people to destruction. John suggests with his imagery that the sword used will be their own. We must be careful not to interpret this "feast" literally, but allow the image of the "feast of the lamb" to give us insight.

In contrast to this "feast" of Satan's warriors is "the marriage of the Lamb" (Revelation 19:7). The righteous Saints are the bride. They too have been gathered, but they have been gathered out of the world by the Savior.

> And I looked, and behold a white cloud, and upon the cloud one sat like unto the Son of man, having on his head a golden crown, and in his hand a sharp sickle.
>
> And another angel came out of the temple, crying with a loud voice to him that sat on the cloud, Thrust in thy sickle, and reap: for the time is come

> for thee to reap; for the harvest of the
> earth is ripe (Revelation 14:14-15). (The
> next verses by contrast allude to the
> gathering of the wicked.)

Those with sealed foreheads are gathered out of all
nations to attend the marriage and the accom-
panying feast of the Lamb. We are told the feast will
consist of the fruit of the tree of life which we know
from Lehi's dream represents the love of God in all
its manifestations.

> In the midst of the street of it,
> and on either side of the river, was
> there the tree of life, which bare twelve
> manner of fruits, and yielded her fruit
> every month: and the leaves of the tree
> were for the healing of the nations
> (Revelation 22:2).

It is a feast of love with full enjoyment of the great
truths of the gospel. Those who partake of the feast
will drink of the pure "river of water of life, clear as
crystal" (Revelation 22:1). The nations under the
mark of the beast have "drunk of the wine of the
wrath of her fornication" (Revelation 18:3). At the
river of life there is quenching of eternal thirst for
the righteous.   By contrast, the wicked are
"scorched with great heat..." as a result of which
"they   gnawed   their   tongues   for   pain"
(Revelation 16:9-10).   In an earlier verse this
contrast of thirst and heat is heightened.

They [the righteous] shall
hunger no more, neither thirst any
more; neither shall the sun light on
them, nor any heat.

For the Lamb which is in the
midst of the throne shall feed them,
and shall lead them unto living
fountains of waters: and God shall
wipe away all tears from their eyes
(Revelation 7:16–17).

The Bride and the Harlot—New Jerusalem and Babylon

The feast images lead us naturally to the two
main images that dominate the last half of the
Revelation. One of these images is a woman (the
bride), the other, a city. They are closely associated.
In chapter twelve we are introduced to "the bride of
Christ."

And there appeared a great
wonder in heaven; a woman clothed
with the sun, and the moon under her
feet, and upon her head a crown of
twelve stars (Revelation 12:1).

The woman, we learn in the Joseph Smith
Translation, represents the Church. She is with
child "travailing in birth" (Revelation 12:2). The
child is the kingdom of God which the Church
seeks to establish. The woman is clothed with the
sun in celestial glory, and crowned with the twelve
Apostles who guide her. The image is one of purity

and beauty, emphasizing the sacrifice and devoted love of motherhood. The woman is radiant because she has kept herself clean for her husband. She reflects his celestial glory. The rest of the chapter deals with the dragon's efforts to destroy the child and smother it during the premortal existence and the various ages of the world. In the twenty–first chapter the imagery of a bride adorned for her husband is continued.

> And I John saw the holy city, new Jerusalem, coming down from God out of heaven, prepared as a bride adorned for her husband (Revelation 21:2).

In verse nine an angel tells John to come with him. "I will shew thee the bride, the Lamb's wife" (Revelation 21:9). The bride image is thus tied to the city image. The image of a bride is a fitting image for Christ's church. It is built on the love that exists between a new bride and her husband. Christ, as the husband, loves and sacrifices for his bride. The bride in turn, is faithful and gives all her love and devotion in return.

We then see "that great city, the holy Jerusalem, descending out of heaven from God, Having the glory of God: and her light was like unto a stone most precious...clear as crystal;" (Revelation 21:10–11). The city, as the woman of chapter twelve, radiates the light of her king. John continues with his description. The beauty of the walls and gates are detailed. The walls symbolize safety and security. They are built upon the

foundation of the Apostles. The gates, named for
the twelve tribes, symbolize the need to enter the city
of God through the house of Israel, either by
adoption or birth. This comes about through the
Abrahamic covenant. That covenant states:

> And I will bless them that bless
> thee, and curse them that curse thee;
> and in thee (that is, in thy Priesthood)
> and in thy seed (that is, thy
> Priesthood), for I give unto thee a
> promise that this right shall continue
> in thee, and in thy seed after thee (that
> is to say, the literal seed, or the seed of
> the body) shall all the families of the
> earth be blessed, even with the
> blessings of the gospel, which are the
> blessings of salvation, even of life
> eternal (Abraham 2:11).

By fulfilling this promise to bless the nations with
"the blessing of salvation, even life eternal," one
becomes worthy to enter his city through the
covenant lineage of Abraham. This is an obvious
reference to the great missionary effort, temple
work, etc. of the Church. By accomplishing it, and
perfecting oneself an individual becomes a true
descendent of Abraham and can enter the city of
God through those gates. A covenant child of
Abraham must share the blessings they have
received with all the world. This is an important
part of the gathering and sealing seen earlier in the
Revelation.

John continues his description with a reference to the city as a temple.

> And I saw no temple therein: for the Lord God Almighty and the Lamb are the temple of it.
> And the city had no need of the sun...for the glory of God did lighten it...
> And the nations...shall walk in the light of it (Revelation 21:21–24).

The description continues with the "river of water of life" and the "tree of life," all depicting the purity and radiance which is fitting for the bride of Christ.

Next to this picture of purity, radiance, fidelity, motherhood, security, love, etc., we place the carnal mirror of Satan. He too has covenants, but his covenants are self–seeking, bringing the destruction of the earth, not the blessing of all nations. He seeks to spread his apostate doctrines and gather his followers. He too has a "bride" and a city that are closely associated. In chapter seventeen we are introduced to "the great whore that sitteth upon many waters: With whom the kings of the earth have committed fornication, and the inhabitants of the earth have been made drunk with the wine of her fornication" (Revelation. 17:1–2). The woman sits on the "scarlet–coloured beast full of names of blasphemy." She is:

> ...arrayed in purple and scarlet colour, and decked with gold and precious stones and pearls, having a

golden cup in her hand full of
abominations and filthiness of her
fornication:

And upon her forehead was a
name written, MYSTERY, BABYLON
THE GREAT, THE MOTHER OF
HARLOTS AND ABOMINATIONS OF
THE EARTH (Revelation 17:4–5).

We are told later in the same chapter:

And the woman which thou
sawest is that great city, which
reigneth over the kings of the earth
(Revelation 17:18).

The city is then described in chapter eighteen. It is
"the habitation of devils and the hold of every foul
spirit" (Revelation 18:2). It is a city of wealth and
decadence, fornication, and drunkenness. Some
interpret this as Rome, but it is clear the city is
spiritual Babylon, meaning wickedness, decadence,
and apostasy in many different forms. At one time
it may have been Rome, but the cities change with
the rising of new powers.

The distortions are obvious. The bride of
Christ is placed opposite the whore of all the earth.
Fidelity is compared to fornication. She is decked
out in purple and scarlet, gaudily covered with
precious stones and pearls. The church of Christ is
clothed with the sun in celestial glory. Since we
know the interpretation of the woman and child of
Christ's kingdom, we can understand the meaning
of the "whore of all the earth." This is Satan's

"church," preaching his gospel and his doctrines. It is a church of apostasy seeking the things of the world with the "kings." The whole of apostate Christianity is encompassed in the image as is all of apostasy in any form. A search of section eighty–six of the Doctrine and Covenants will support this image and interpretation considerably. In this section we have an interpretation of Christ's parable of the wheat and the tares. Notice how verse three links the "whore" and "Babylon" with the apostasy.

> And after they have fallen asleep the great persecutor of the church, the apostate, the whore, even Babylon, that maketh all nations to drink of her cup, in whose hearts the enemy, even Satan, sitteth to reign—behold he soweth the tares; wherefore, the tares choke the wheat and drive the church into the wilderness (D&C 86:3).

This verse casts additional light on the image of Christ's bride (the church) as explained in chapter twelve. We have seen in chapter twelve that the red dragon stood ready to devour the child the woman is about to deliver. Eventually the woman is chased into the wilderness of apostasy. Section eighty–six teaches that this driving of the church into the wilderness is closely associated with "the great persecutor of the church, the apostate, the whore, even Babylon." Other passages in the Doctrine and Covenants speak of the Restoration of the Church as her coming forth out of the wilderness.

> And to none else will I grant this
> power, to receive this same testimony
> among this generation, in this the
> beginning of the rising up and the
> coming forth of my church out of the
> wilderness—clear as the moon, and
> fair as the sun, and terrible as an army
> with banners (D&C 5:14).

Notice the repetition of imagery as found in
Revelation, chapter twelve. Coming out of the
wilderness represents the Restoration. Truth
prevails over a wilderness of apostate doctrines,
creeds and principles.

The great battle between Satan's apostate
ideologies, supported by the "kings" or governments
of the world and the truths of the gospel, is
catalogued. In different ages of the world Babylon,
the whore, etc. take different forms, but their
message and purpose are always the same. They
seek the worship and allegiance owed to Christ and
his bride. A true understanding of the apocalyptic
nature of John's images will prevent a narrow,
limited view, pinpointing to one organization,
church, or interpretation that will blind us to the
real enemies of Christ's kingdom.

The whore of all the earth also has children
which serve as a parallel image to the "child" of the
woman of chapter twelve. However, Satan's
kingdom is one of confusion. As there are many
heads, on the dragon and beast, so his "bride" will
have many children. These many children lead to a
world of confusion, each seeking its own aims, and
profits with their resultant evils. The emphasis

should not be placed on a single organization but on apostasy in all its forms wherever it is found. She is called the "Mother of Harlots and Abominations." She is a harlot because she and her children have left their true husband—Christ—to live with the world. Because they do this for money and power, they have sold themselves.

The woman representing Christ's church seeks to bring forth the kingdom of God. Hence by parallelism Satan seeks through his "mother" to bring forth his kingdom, a kingdom of "mystery," the kingdom of Babylon, a kingdom which seeks to establish the treasures, falsehoods, and power of the world. Mystery and Babylon are written in the forehead of the woman, a pattern we have already seen. The whore clearly belongs to Babylon, the world, and Satan. She boldly bears their names in her forehead. The name of the city of God is written on the foreheads of the righteous as promised in chapter three, verse twelve.

The image relationship of the whore, representing apostasy, to the whole of Satan's kingdom is vividly described by the prophet Joseph Smith in section 123 of the Doctrine and Covenants. Notice what the Prophet indicates is the influence or spirit behind, "murder," "tyranny," "confusion," etc. All the fruits of the red, dark and pale horses are apparent.

> It is an imperative duty that we owe to God, to angels, with whom we shall be brought to stand, and also to ourselves, to our wives and children, who have been made to bow down with

grief, sorrow, and care, under the most
damning hand of murder, tyranny,
and oppression, *supported* and *urged
on* and *upheld by the influence of that
spirit which hath so strongly riveted
the creeds of the fathers, who have
inherited lies,* upon the hearts of the
children, and filled the world with
confusion, and has been growing
stronger and stronger, and *is now the
very mainspring of all corruption,* and
the whole earth groans under the
weight of its iniquity.

It is an iron yoke, it is a strong
band; they are the very handcuffs, and
chains, and shackles, and fetters of
hell (D&C 123:7–8).

Thus we see, Satan's "mother" has become "the
very mainspring of all corruption." Throughout
chapter seventeen the whore of the earth is closely
associated with a seven–headed beast with horns
and crowns. She "sits upon" this beast, but in a
very real way the beast also sits upon her
(Revelation 17:3). We have seen the association of
these two in the Doctrine and Covenants verses
quoted above. Joseph F. Smith speaking in 1914,
during the first World War helps us further
understand the association of apostasy with the
wars and the destructions of the last days.

We know that the spirit of strife
and contention exists to an alarming
extent among all the people of the

world. Why does it exist? Because they are not one with God, nor with Christ. They have not entered into the true fold, and the result is they do not possess the spirit of the true Shepherd sufficiently to govern and control their acts in the ways of peace and righteousness.

...they are members of the same churches, worshipping in the same forms of religion, and yet they are calling upon God one against another, to defend them against their enemies, and to strengthen their arms to destroy their foes. What does it prove? It proves what God said. They have not his Spirit; they have not his power to guide them. They are not in possession of his truth; and therefore, the very conditions that exist are the results of this unbelief in the truth; *and this worship of men and organizations and power of men* is divested of the power of God (*Gospel Doctrine* pp. 417, 419–420).

Could we read a clearer statement describing the power and influence of the images John has given us in Revelation? Can we not see the mark of Satan's beast written all over an apostate world as it existed down through the ages? That apostasy has taken away the deep love that John preached and Christ exemplified. Since it is missing there is no force strong enough to keep men from destroying each other.

The city image can be readily seen without
great commentary.   Opposite Zion—the new
Jerusalem, is Babylon.   The "holy city, new
Jerusalem" is seen "coming down from God out of
heaven" (Revelation 21:2). Babylon, as all of Satan's
dominions throughout Revelation, ascends out of
the bottomless pit. There are no walls of security or
safety, even though the city claims it will continue
forever (Revelation 18:7). After her brief reign she
"is fallen is fallen" (Revelation 18:2). Her final end
is with Satan "cast...into the bottomless pit"
(Revelation 20:3).   The final end of the New
Jerusalem is to dwell with Christ and the Father.
As the nations and kings once gave glory to
Babylon, after her fall and the establishment of the
New Jerusalem they give glory to the celestial city.
The New Jerusalem houses the tree of life and the
river of life. Babylon is the home of "every foul
spirit." The comparisons are practically endless.
Again let us not try to identify Babylon with a single
city. During the history of the earth, Babylon has
been associated with many different seats of power.
The image as an archetype can stand on its own
and be applied to many different societies and
civilizations.

A Final Comparison

These are some examples of the beauty and
depth of John's symbolic imagery. It can provide
keys to understanding the Revelation. One last
parallel can serve as a capstone phrase to conclude
John's imagery. Satan's "beast that thou sawest
was, and is not; and shall ascend out of the

bottomless pit, and *go into perdition*" (Revelation 17:8). This is a marvelous contrasting parallel to the following praise rendered to God. "We give thee thanks, O Lord God Almighty *which art, and wast,* and *art to come...*" (Revelation 11:17). Satan "*was*" and "*is not*" and shall "*go into perdition.*" Christ "*is*" (art) and "*was*" and *will* "*come*" to reign.

An Open Door

There is one final parallel image I would like to mention. It is not a distorted mirror of Satan but a comparison drawn between the Savior and an individual. It is a paired image that causes reflection and creates a deeper love for Christ. It acts as a catalyst to help us choose the selfless humility of Christ not the selfish pride of Satan. We mentioned earlier that Christ had certain keys and that he opened doors with those keys. His keys open the door to the bottomless pit, frees the prisoners there from death and hell, and then opens the door to the celestial city and throne of God. In the message to Philadelphia, Christ makes the following statement that is a fitting description of all he does, "I have set before thee an open door, and no man can shut it..." (Revelation 3:8). This is the image of Christ's door. It is always open through the power of his Atonement. It will remain open; no one has the power to shut it. We can refuse to walk through it for that is our agency, but it's passageway will never be closed to the truly repentant.

In the latter part of this same chapter we see another door. This is the door to our hearts, our kingdom. John describes it in the following manner. Christ is speaking.

> Behold, I stand at the door, and knock: if any man hear my voice, and open the door, I will come in to him, and will sup with him, and he with me (Revelation 3:20).

Our doors are often shut and with true humility the Savior comes to us seeking entrance. His door is always open; ours require his gentle knock. The truest humility is not when we seek entrance to his table in meek recognition of his higher station. The truest humility is when he, a being of obvious superiority, condescends to knock at our doors and "sup" at our tables. It is this same being that invites all to "sit with me in my throne" (Revelation 3:21). Is it any wonder that John concludes his Revelation with a prayer that Christ will come, not with the warning, not to add or take from his writing. That warning is present but it does not hold the power of John's concluding statements. The power comes with John's prayer and invitation. John contemplates the misery and sorrow Satan has brought in all periods of the earth's history and the future sorrows he knows will come. He also sees the peace and beauty of the New Jerusalem. With these two great contrasts in mind John issues his prayer to the Master.

> And the Spirit and bride say,
> Come. And let him that heareth say,
> Come. And let him that is athirst
> come. And whosoever will, let him
> take the water of life freely (Revelation
> 22:17).

Christ then promises, "Surely I come quickly. Amen." To which John replies: "Even so, come, Lord Jesus" (Revelation 22:20). His coming will shatter the twisted mirror while all will acknowledge the true King of the Earth.